MW00988355

Wake Up, Wake Up, to Do the Work of the Creator

WILLIAM B. HELMREICH

WAKE UP, WAKE UP, TO DO THE WORK OF THE CREATOR

HARPER & ROW, PUBLISHERS

NEW YORK, HAGERSTOWN, SAN FRANCISCO, LONDON

FIRST EDITION

Designed by Patricia Girvin Dunbar

Library of Congress Cataloging in Publication Data

Helmreich, William B
  Wake up, wake up, to do the work of the creator.

  1. Helmreich, William B. 2. Orthodox Judaism—
United States—Biography. 3. Jewish way of life.
4. New York (City)—Biography. I. Title.
BM755.H33A33 1976   974.7'1'04924024 [B]   76–5129
ISBN 0–06–011823–7

76 77 78 79 80 10 9 8 7 6 5 4 3 2 1

To
Mark and Norma

SPECIAL THANKS

To my wife, Helaine, who gave not only encouragement and support but also many valuable suggestions and insightful observations. Whatever merit this book possesses owes a great deal to her.

To my parents, Leo and Sally Helmreich, and my brother, Mark.

To my editor, Virginia Hilu, who gave me self-confidence and inspiration; Professor Sid Z. Leiman, whose meticulous review of the manuscript clarified my thinking in a number of areas relating to Jewish history and law; and to Chava Miller, who, in addition to typing the book carefully and intelligently, contributed numerous helpful and thought-provoking comments.

And, finally, to the various people who appear in the book. Without them it could never have been written.

Wake Up, Wake Up, to Do the Work of the Creator

Tuesday morning we walked down the steps leading to the boarding gate at the Port Authority Bus Terminal on Forty-first Street between Eighth and Ninth Avenues.

We arrived at the gate. The suitcases were already being loaded onto the red and silver Trailways bus that stood nearby. With my father's help, I carried my bags over to the rectangular-shaped baggage hold in the side of the bus. The porter took them and pushed them all the way in.

People were starting to board. I turned around to say goodbye to my parents. My mother was crying softly. My father's eyes looked watery and I had great difficulty swallowing. "Don't worry, Daddy," I said, my voice quavering. "I'll be good. You don't have to worry about me." "I know," replied my father. "It's just that you and Mark are all we have and we're going to miss you. Still, I feel that this is the right thing and we want to do what's best for you." "I wish Mark was here," I thought. "He'd probably kid around and then maybe I wouldn't feel so bad." My brother, Mark, was six years my senior and had a full-time job. Unfortunately, he had been unable to get off from work and I had had to say goodbye to him in the morning. My father's voice broke in on my reflections: "Willy, I have great hopes for you, that you will learn well, and always be a G-d-fearing Jew. Don't forget what you learned."

Suddenly, I became afraid. "But it's such a good yeshiva.

1

What if I can't keep up with the other boys? What if they don't like the way I learn? And the hours are so long." "Don't worry," answered my father. "Remember what the Talmud tells us: If a man says, 'I didn't look and I found,' don't believe him. If he says, 'I looked and I didn't find,' don't believe him either; but if a man says, 'I looked and I found'—then you can believe him." Putting his hands on my shoulders, my father continued: "I have no doubt that you can succeed. You just have to want to badly enough. Now hurry, the bus is getting ready to leave."

Looking around, I saw that he was right. The platform was deserted. I bent down, kissed my parents, went out the glass door and boarded the bus. I found a seat in the back on the right side so that I could see my parents. They were still there, of course, their loving faces pressed against the window, hands waving to me. From the height of the bus they appeared much smaller. How lonely they looked, standing out there by themselves. I suddenly realized how much I meant to them and they to me. Letting me leave home was not easy for them. All the evenings spent studying the Talmud with my father flashed through my mind, all preparation, as it turned out, for the future, the future that was now here.

As the bus pulled out, their figures became tinier until they appeared as mere dots. Finally, even those were no longer visible. The bus rumbled through the few city blocks that led to the Lincoln Tunnel. As we entered the tunnel and the inside of the bus became dark, I fervently said the prayer that every Orthodox Jew is supposed to recite as he begins a journey:

May it be Thy will, Lord our G-d and G-d of our fathers, to lead us in safety and to direct our every step in safety.

May Thou bring us to our destination in life, happiness and peace.

Save us from every enemy and ambush and from all the thieves and wild animals that lurk on the road and from all afflictions that visit and trouble the world.

Send a blessing upon the work of Thy hands.

Let me acquire grace, loving-kindness and mercy in Thine eyes and in the eyes of all who see us.

Hear our pleas, for Thou art the Lord, who listens to our prayers and to our pleas.

Blessed art Thou, O Lord, who hears our prayers.

In our house the Sabbath was

the most important day of the week. Preparations began on Wednesday, when my mother would take me to the butcher. Like so many of the Orthodox Jews in the area, Mr. Lupowitz was a refugee. He had come to America after World War II. His store was on the ground floor of a six-story tenement building, whose brick structure had weathered to a shade of dull gold.

On the left side as one walked in stood the display case, which was almost bare. One asked Mr. Lupowitz for a veal steak or chicken and he would go into the "box," or refrigerator, and bring out the meat. The wooden floor was covered with sawdust. My most vivid memories are of Mr. Lupowitz giving me two or three slices of salami and telling me to "be a good boy and play nicely so your mother will have naches

[joy] from you." My mother, in the meantime, would usually be sitting on a hard-back, plastic-covered chair chatting with some of the other customers. We seldom spent less than an hour there. My mother, and all the other customers for that matter, would always reject the first cuts of meat that were brought out and Mr. Lupowitz would then go back and return with another selection. Sometimes this would happen five or six times. I would usually play ball in front of the store, running in now and then to see if I could get some more salami from Mr. Lupowitz.

On Thursday night my mother would be up late cooking for the Sabbath. The cream-colored, Formica-top kitchen table would be covered with brown paper, upon which lay the chicken, already chopped into pieces. My mother would drop these pieces into the large metal pot with the two handles. Soon the aroma of fresh soup began to pervade our four-room apartment. How I loved that smell! Perhaps it was because we had chicken only on the Sabbath, but more probable was the fact that this smell unofficially ushered in the holiday.

On Friday afternoon the entire family came home early. The yeshiva was in session for only half a day and my father left work about two or three hours before the Sabbath was to begin. He would always quote the following saying to me when I asked him why we had to be home so early, why one hour before the Sabbath would be too late: "Those who hallow the Sabbath end it late and begin early." My father simply could not wait until the Sabbath began. He would shave and shower quickly and then urge Mark and me on: "Boys, you'll be late for Shabbos. Don't forget to brush your shoes. Did you prepare your suits?" Finally, we would all be ready, shoes polished, wearing our starched white shirts and pressed suits, ready to leave for the evening service at the synagogue.

4

As the sun began to set, my mother would light four Sabbath candles, one for each member of our family. She would then cover her eyes with her hands and say the appropriate blessing. Following this she would stand still for a few moments murmuring private prayers for the welfare of our family. We all stood silently waiting for her to finish. Finally, opening her eyes, my mother would say, "Gut Shabbos." "Gut Shabbos," we would answer. The Sabbath had begun.

There was something exquisite in that ceremony. One could sense in it the quiet of the approaching Sabbath, which above all meant rest and closeness to G-d. The house was silent; no radio could be played, no telephone answered, no light turned on or off, for any use of electricity was considered work. The candles would eventually burn themselves out, and our home would be darkened and serene.

When we left our apartment for the evening services, we would walk down the five flights of stairs, for the restriction against using electricity forbade us to take the elevator. Of course, as we passed through the apartment door, we would kiss the mezuzah, which was there because the Torah had commanded: ". . . you shall write them on the doorposts of your house and on your gates" (Deuteronomy 6:9). Inside the mezuzah were two Biblical passages written on a small scroll of parchment: "Hear, O Israel, the Lord is our G-d, the Lord is One" (Deuteronomy 6:4) and "And if you will carefully obey my commandments . . ." (Deuteronomy 11:13). To others, the mezuzah might have been only a sign that this was a Jewish home, but for us it was a reminder of G-d's presence and of our duties to obey Him.

As we walked to the synagogue, people, quite a few of them Jewish, were coming home from work, but work was the furthest thing from our minds. I was already trying to guess what melody the cantor would use for the prayer that welcomed the Sabbath.

We climbed the narrow, faded-marble stairs, walked through the door into the synagogue, or shul, and entered a world vastly different from the outside. Mr. Verba, our part-time beadle or sexton, had polished the candelabra and dusted off the lights. Whatever could be done to brighten up the large room had been done. Even the metal plates nailed to the benches, upon which were engraved the seat numbers, had been shined up a bit. Here and there were some telltale signs of neglect: a small hole in the mechitzah, or curtain that separated the men from the women, a few burnt-out bulbs on the memorial wall plaques, and a bench that had come loose from its mooring. Through the beadle's efforts, a clear difference had been established between the Sabbath and the rest of the week. Each distinction enabled us to feel the significance of the Sabbath a bit more, and to share our inner peace with that which was around us.

The synagogue was located on the second floor of a three-story walk-up. The first floor consisted of commercial stores, and the third, empty for several years, was now rented out to a political club.

A small section in the rear of the synagogue was reserved for women. It was separated from where the men sat by a flimsy white curtain. The floor was covered with old linoleum whose design had long since been rubbed out by the shoes of the worshipers. The monotony of the ugly beige-brown walls was broken by patches where pieces of paint had come off. At the front of the synagogue and stretching the length of the room on the right side were several wide but not tall windows partially covered by a gray glaze, on which was painted a black Star of David with the name of our synagogue in the center: "Tifereth Israel" or "Glory of

Israel" congregation. Naked fluorescent bulbs hung from a gray ceiling.

An unimposing place perhaps, and yet to me my synagogue was more beautiful than the larger ones in our neighborhood. Our synagogue was "heimish," a place where one felt comfortable, where you knew everyone and they knew you.

Facing the congregation was the Holy Ark, inside of which were the Torahs, the sacred scrolls. This was the focal point of the room, the part which gave the synagogue life and color. Everyone faced toward the Ark. To turn one's back on the Ark was considered a sign of disrespect for the Holy Scrolls that stood inside. Moreover, the synagogue had been built so that the Ark faced east, in the direction of Jerusalem. Despite the thousands of miles that separated us from that holy city, I always felt I had moved one step closer to it by thinking about what lay beyond the Ark itself.

"I have placed the Lord before me forever" was the inscription above the Ark, in gold-painted wrought-iron Hebrew letters. On each side of that inscription was a lion, the Biblical symbol of the tribe of Judah, which with the tribe of Levi comprised the only two tribes that had not been lost when the Jews went into exile almost two thousand years ago. The Ark was covered by a purple velvet curtain on which was stitched in gold thread the first few words of each of the Ten Commandments. The Ark was opened only when the Torah was taken out for the weekly reading and when it was replaced. To reach it, one had to walk up three low steps.

All is silent. The cantor slowly walks to the front and, facing the Ark, begins the chant with the melody whose familiar strains always brought forth in me anticipation mixed with the security of knowing what was coming. "O come let us exult before the Lord. Let us shout for joy to the Rock of our salvation." "Yes, yes, let us do so. The Sabbath is here," I thought as I repeated the opening line and went on with the prayer: "For the Lord is a great G-d and a great King above all gods. . . . Oh, that ye would listen to His voice!" Each of us went at his own pace, but the cantor waited until all had finished before completing the prayer. More prayers said. More preliminary praises to G-d, and then my favorite prayer, the one which began: "Come, my friend, to greet the bride, let us welcome the presence of the Sabbath." The prayer consisted of nine stanzas welcoming the Sabbath, the last of which is: "Come in peace, crown of thy husband, with rejoicing and with cheerfulness, in the midst of the faithful of the chosen people. Come, O bride; come, O bride." As we said these last words, all would bow down, first to one side and then to the other.

Each week the Sabbath was new and special and each week we welcomed it in this manner.

Outside we could hear the bus pulling away from the stop near 106th Street and Broadway, the same stop that my mother and I would wait at on those occasions, during the week, when we left Manhattan's Upper West Side and went downtown to shop. The lights of the apartment building across the street became visible as the colors in the sky shifted from the dark gray of twilight to the black of night. Inside, the cantor was intoning, as everyone rose, the Biblical passage:

> And the children of Israel shall keep the Sabbath,
> to observe the Sabbath throughout their generations,
> as an everlasting covenant.
> It is a sign between me and the children of Israel forever,

that in six days the Lord made the heavens and the earth
and on the seventh day he rested,
and ceased from his work.

Exodus 31:16–17

My father had once said to me that if G-d, who had the
capacity to create an entire world, had needed to rest, how
much truer was this of mere mortals. From my perspective,
I thought we were fortunate to have a special holiday every
seventh day of the week. I had a feeling of being part of the
Creation, of actually having been there because I was resting
in the same way that G-d had.

When we leave, night has fallen. We say "Gut Shabbos"
to everyone in shul whom we know, or whose glance meets
ours, making certain not to forget the rabbi. As we walk
home, the stars look peaceful and I feel closer to them. The
passing cars seem distant, not merely because I would not
dream of riding in one on the Sabbath, but also because I
know hardly anyone who would. My friends are all Orthodox, and the same is true, more or less, of my parents'
friends.

Rudy's candy store with all the airplane models in the
window is still open as we go by, but I don't even stop to
look, for we are forbidden to use money on the Sabbath and
cannot, therefore, buy anything. My father enters the apartment building first and removes his keys from his suspend-
ers, where he has fastened them. His handkerchief is there,
too, for one may not carry anything in the public domain on
the Sabbath more than four paces. As the key turns, I can
hear footsteps approaching. My mother is coming. "Gut
Shabbos," she says, opening the door.

We all file into the living room and begin singing "Sholem

Aleichem" ("Peace be unto you"), the song that marks the opening of the Sabbath meal.

> Peace be with you ministering angels,
> angels of the most high.
> From the king of kings,
> the Holy One, the blessed one.

That was the first stanza of the hymn, a hymn that was sung to the tune of a melody that had been sung in my grandparents' home in Europe, and which on that evening was being sung in hundreds of thousands of homes throughout the world. I was anchored; I had a past. Although I might be nothing more than a speck on the map of Jewish history, the shape and location of that map were clear in my mind. I belonged—and every ceremony that we performed, every prayer I said, strengthened that image. When I went to a friend's house for Shabbos and heard the same melodies, uttered the same benedictions and even ate the same foods, I felt a bond that tied me inseparably to my people.

The table was set in the traditional Sabbath manner. At the head where my father sat were two braided challahs (loaves of bread), which symbolized the double portion of the manna that the Israelites had gathered on the sixth day of the week and that had to last them through the Sabbath. The challahs were covered by a satin cloth with yellow fringes upon which were stitched the words "In Honor of the Sabbath." To the right sat a silver wine cup with a Star of David engraved on the side. The candles, burning brightly, stood on the opposite end of the table. The tablecloth was solid white, simple yet elegant.

After "Sholem Aleichem," my father turned to my mother and said the prayer "A Woman of Worth," whose words had been written by King Solomon himself:

A good wife who can find?
  She is far more precious than jewels.
The heart of her husband trusts in her.
  And he will never lack gain.
She does him good, and not harm,
  all the days of her life.
She seeks wool and flax,
  and works with willing hands.
She is like the ships of the merchant,
  from far away, she brings her food.
She rises while it is still night
  and provides food for her household
  and tasks for her maidens.
She considers a field and buys it;
  with the fruit of her hands she plants a vineyard.
She girds her loins with strength
  and makes her arms strong.
She perceives that her merchandise is profitable.
  Her lamp does not go out at night.
She sets her hand to the distaff,
  and her hands hold the spindle.
She stretches forth her hand to the poor,
  and reaches out her hands to the needy.
She is not afraid of snow for her household,
  for all her household are clothed in scarlet.
She makes herself coverings;
  her clothing is fine linen and scarlet.
Her husband is known in the gates,
  when he sits among the elders of the land.
She makes linen garments and sells them;
  she supplies girdles to the merchant.
Honor and dignity are her clothing,
  and she laughs at the time to come.
She opens her mouth with wisdom,
  and the teaching of kindness is on her tongue.
She looks well to the ways of her household,

and never eats the bread of idleness.
Her children rise up and bless her;
    her husband also praises her:
"Many women have done excellently,
    but you exceed them all."
Charm is deceptive and beauty is vain,
    but a woman who fears the Lord is to be praised.
Give her of the fruit of her hands,
    and let her works praise her in the gates.

Proverbs 31:10–31

Another prayer was said by my father as we all stood at the table in the living room. Placing one hand on my head, the other on my brother's, he would say: "G-d render thee like Ephraim and Manasseh." (To a daughter, one would say: "G-d render thee like Sarah, Rebecca, Rachel and Leah.")

Then my father would fill the cup to the brim with wine and begin saying the Kiddush, the blessing over the wine. After he finished, we answered "Amen," and my mother, Mark and I would each make the same blessing and then go into the kitchen to wash our hands. I had learned in school that a table filled with the Lord's food was comparable to the Holy Altar in the Temple. And could one conceive of approaching the altar with unclean hands? After my father, mother and Mark had washed their hands, I filled the glass with water, first pouring the water over my right hand, then over my left, making certain that the water reached my wrists, as prescribed by law. My brother would give me a towel to dry my hands, but before I did so I would say: "Blessed art Thou, Lord our G-d, King of the Universe, who has sanctified us with His commandments and commanded us concerning the washing of the hands."

We dried our hands and returned to the table, at which point my father would say, "Blessed art Thou, Lord our G-d, King of the Universe, who brings forth bread from the earth." He then cut the challah with a long silver serrated knife, and after salting each piece lightly, gave a piece to each of us.

My mother always made a special effort for the Sabbath meal. We had fresh fillet of sole, cold with mayonnaise on it, after which my father would raise his wine cup and exclaim, "Le Chaim" ("To Life"), and drink from it. Following that came my favorite part, the singing of songs to honor the Sabbath and make it a joyous occasion. Most of the poems, written in medieval times, proclaimed the glory of the Sabbath.

Naturally, we said grace at the conclusion of every meal, but Sabbath was different. First we sang every part aloud, unhurriedly, for we wanted to beautify the Sabbath through song. Second, we prefaced the grace with the 126th Psalm:

A SONG OF ASCENTS

When the Lord brought back those who returned to Zion,
we were as in a dream.

Then was our mouth filled with laughter
and our tongue with joyous song,
then said they among the nations,
the Lord has done great things for them.

The Lord has done great things for us,
joyful we were.

Lord turn back our captivity,
as streams to arid soil.

They who sow in tears
shall reap in joy.

Though he goes forth weeping, who bears the trailing seed, with song of joy shall he come home, bearing his sheaves.

Prayers such as these made me aware that my people had endured suffering, but that it was all for a purpose and part of G-d's will, a will whose motives I could not fathom yet had to accept. The substance of this prayer was supported wherever I turned. On top of the oak dresser in my parents' bedroom was a tin charity box for a yeshiva (a Hebrew school) in Israel, the same Israel that the Psalm referred to when it said, "Lord, turn back our captivity." In school when we were asked to donate a dollar, we received a certificate with a tree drawn on it, acknowledging that the bearer now owned one tree in Israel. The importance of a foot of land in Alaska I had acquired from a breakfast cereal company paled when compared to a piece of the Holy Land. Did I not mention the word "Israel" at least fifty times a day in my prayers? Was this not the home of Abraham, Isaac and Jacob, the very reason for which we had been delivered out of Egypt?

After supper, my father studied the weekly reading that was to be said the following day in synagogue. Painstakingly, with love caressing every word, my father would read aloud: "In the beginning G-d created the heaven and the earth. . . . And G-d said: 'Let there be light,' and there was light." My father would read the Hebrew and then translate, adding the explanations of various commentaries to further clarify the passages.

As my father talked, the candles began to flicker and go out one by one. I used to gaze into them, finding the blue center, and creating images of the Biblical scenes my father was describing. Here was Noah sailing away to safety in his

14

specially constructed ark. Or there was Moses on Mount Sinai receiving the Torah from our Maker.

Gradually the living room became dark. Then all the lights, save the ones in the kitchen and bathroom, went out. The Sabbath clock was attached to the electricity in the house. The lights could be set to go off at any time. Since we did not actually turn off the lights, we had not violated the Sabbath. The following day the lights would go on again as darkness set in.

My father closed the Chumash (Pentateuch) in the now dimly lit room, bade me "Gut Shabbos" and went to bed. As I sat down on my bed, I said the last prayer of the day:

> Blessed art Thou, Lord our G-d, King of the Universe,
> who weighs down my eyes with the bonds of sleep,
> my eyelids with slumber.
>
> Lord my G-d, G-d of my fathers,
> may it be Thy will to lay me down in peace,
> and to raise me up again in peace.
>
> May the thoughts that come to me,
> disturbing dreams and evil fancies, not trouble me,
> but grant that my rest be perfect before Thee.
>
> Lighten my eyes again lest I sleep the sleep of death.
> Blessed art Thou, Lord, whose glory gives light
>   to the whole universe.

The day had ended. The shadows of Moses and Abraham moved across the walls. No longer permitted to speak, eat or drink, I closed my eyes and fell asleep.

Sabbath morning had a

special quality about it. On other mornings I would awaken to the sound of the seven o'clock news. On the Sabbath morning, however, all was still. My father, always a punctual man, was especially concerned that we not be late for services.

By the time we were dressed, a glass of tea and a piece of cake were waiting on the table for Mark and me. We did not eat a full breakfast, because we had not yet prayed.

With my father urging us on—"Hurry up or we'll be late" —we finished, put on our coats and began the three-block walk to the synagogue, I on my father's left, my brother on his right. As I walked through the streets, I would often think about how different we were from the other residents of the neighborhood, an area that was changing from one predominantly Jewish, Irish and Italian to one that was Puerto Rican and Black.

I had been made conscious of being different in a hundred different ways, ranging from the way people looked at me to insults and taunts. I used to play with a gang of boys on the block—Richie, Mikey, Paul and others, whose faces have long since blurred. Until I was six these were my friends.

Our paths diverged abruptly when I began attending the Hebrew day school two blocks from my house and my friends began public school. I can still remember the look on my friends' faces. One day my mother had come to school to pick me up, and as we walked by the gray tenement house in front of which the boys usually lounged, one of them yelled, "Hey, Willy! C'mon, wanna play stoop ball?" "I can't right now," I answered weakly. My mother had already told me that I could no longer play with them, saying something suspiciously vague about "doing your homework." A few days later I began to understand.

I had accompanied my mother to the grocery store, where I bumped into Richie and Mikey.

"Hey, how come you can't play with us no more?"

"My mother won't let me," I responded.

Mikey gave me a funny look. "How come you don't go to our school?"

"I don't know," I said, beginning to feel uncomfortable. I looked around for my mother, but she was in another part of the store.

"Where do you go to school?"

"Down the block," I answered, pointing in the direction of my school.

Richie and Mikey looked at me in silence for about a minute. Then, as though I were not there, Richie said to Mikey, "He goes to the Jew school." "Yeah," said Mikey, "that's where they all go, those guys with the beanies on their heads."

Suddenly, without warning, Mikey gave me a hard shove, saying at the same time, "Dirty Jew bastard." I fell back among some cartons that were lying in the aisle. At that moment my mother appeared and the boys scattered.

I walked home in a daze. My mother seemed unaware of what had transpired.

"Mommy, Mikey called me a dirty Jew," I said plaintively.

17

"I told you, Willy, from now on you don't play with those boys. You'll have your own friends at school."

We never played together again.

> By the mouth of the upright Thou art praised.
> By the words of the righteous Thou art blessed.
> By the tongue of the faithful Thou art exalted.
> In the midst of the holy Thou art sanctified.

These words were part of a prayer that was said only on Sabbath morning. In a sense it set the tone for the rest of the service. Shortly after these words were uttered, the congregation would rise as the cantor bowed his head low to the Ark and intoned, "Bless the Lord, who is blessed," and the congregation said in unison, also with bowed heads, "Blessed be the Lord, who is blessed forever and ever." From then on no one was permitted to talk until the end of the Amidah (the prayer said standing). During this half-hour we said the most important prayers of the Sabbath service, including the Shema, a portion from the Old Testament itself that sets forth G-d's commandments to the children of Israel to obey Him and which was recited at least twice a day by all Orthodox Jews.

Unlike in other, more formal synagogues, the prayers were said aloud and spontaneously. Mr. Rosenbaum walked slowly back and forth, clapping his hands (about every fourth step) and saying: "Enlighten our eyes in Thy Torah, attach our hearts to Thy commandments." Mr. Pincus would stand in a corner, his prayer shawl over his head, trying to shut out the world that was apparently affecting his concentration, saying: "O bring us home in peace from the four corners of the earth, and allow us to walk upright to our land, for Thou art the G-d who performs victories."

And Mr. Mazer—who can forget him as he sat all alone in a corner near the back, his muscles tense and his fists balled up as though he were trying literally to squeeze the emotion out of his frail, aged body and send it winging heavenward? "Our Father, merciful Father, Thou who art full of compassion, take pity on us and help us to understand and discern, to listen, learn and teach, to observe, do and fulfill all the teachings of Thy Torah."

These words, all part of the same prayer, were being said at the same time. To have said each prayer in unison would have inhibited the freedom of expression that enabled us to pray with fervor. Besides, certain words meant more to different people, and at different times, depending on their mood.

If one could judge from outward appearances, most of the congregants in the synagogue were unexceptional people. Mr. Rosenbaum was an unskilled laborer in the garment industry. Mr. Pincus owned a small butcher shop, and Mr. Mazer was an order clerk for a Wall Street brokerage firm. But on the Sabbath they were kings. Dressed in their finest clothes, their worn shoes polished to a high gloss, they stood and walked erect. Here in the synagogue they communicated with their Maker, received honors as they were dispensed by the gabbai (an administrative official of the synagogue), talked, sang, argued, and dreamed of a day when all wrongs would be righted, all mistakes forgiven, all misfortunes overcome. A day when they would receive their reward for having shown faith in G-d and for having adhered to the faith of their forefathers Abraham, Isaac, Jacob.

For many of these people, recent immigrants from Hitler's inferno, the shtetl still lived. Its way of life continued to influence them as they crowded around the Kiddush table after services for a schnapps and some egg kichel or herring.

They lived in the past despite its recent horrors and turned to the future only for the sake of their children.

My father's parents, for example, had been brutally murdered by the Nazis. How had it happened? No surprises there. In the small village in eastern Poland where my grandparents lived, anti-Semitism had long been a way of life among the local inhabitants. My grandparents were hiding in a cellar along with about fifty other Jews. They had almost made it, for it was 1944. But a hungry peasant boy, whose parents had known my family for many years and had been on good terms with them, betrayed their hiding place for a piece of bread. The Nazis came. The group was led to a field on the outskirts of the village, forced to dig their own graves, and then shot like so many ducks in a shooting gallery.

Frequently, I would ask my father how he had managed to retain his faith through the years before he came to America, and he would say: "To believe in G-d when all is well is no accomplishment. If we really see G-d as all-powerful and admit to not understanding His ways, then we must accept what He does without questioning."

The shul had no board of directors, no president and no vice president. There were no monthly or even annual meetings. It was run by Rabbi Levy, who was its spiritual leader. With his long black beard flecked with gray and his double-breasted long black coat, he was a commanding figure. His mournful brown eyes and limping walk conveyed the impression of a man who had suffered.

Although not wealthy, he was not poor either and gave liberally to support the shul. Some money was raised through sporadic appeals, but the majority of the members were men of little means. Years ago the rabbi, who had originally come to America through Palestine, had had a rich congregation, one of the wealthiest in the community, but his tendency toward bluntness and his fierce pride often got him into hot water. He had, on one memorable occasion, told some wealthy supporters of the synagogue who were busy talking during the Torah reading: "If you want to talk, go outside. This is not the place for it." Offended, these people left the shul. A more prudent person might have kept quiet rather than alienate his most lucrative source of support, but not Rabbi Levy. He was a man who spoke his mind and let the chips fall where they may.

Every Sabbath morning the following ritual would be enacted:

"Mr. Friesel," Rabbi Levy would say, "go up and say Shachris [the morning service]."

"No, ask someone else."

"Why don't you go up?"

"No, I really can't. I have a sore throat." (Clearing his throat several times.)

"Do us a favor, Mr. Friesel, we'd like to hear you."

"All right," the man would say, slowly moving toward the front where the cantor stood. In reality, he had been flattered at being asked. In fact, he had so enjoyed the flattery that he had refused several times so that he could be asked again.

Sometimes a person would genuinely not wish to be the cantor or would refuse so many times that he would overplay his hand. The rabbi would then continue to ask around until someone finally consented. True, there were some people who said yes immediately, but these persons were usually strangers, unaware that such machinations were part of shtibl, or small synagogue, politics, just as giving a kiddush, or small party, after services, or the presenting of a cover for the Ark, was a political and social event.

Once when I was thirteen, the rabbi asked me to lead the services. I declined, saying I had a cold. The following week I still was feeling somewhat under the weather, and again said no. Apparently, the rabbi must have thought it somewhat nervy that I, a thirteen-year-old, should refuse his request, for he became visibly angry. "Let me know when you don't have a cold," he snapped, stalking off. Actually, I had not been playing games, yet it took some doing before I was finally able to convince him of this.

The synagogue was a place where things happened, where people showed emotion, where people had different personalities and quirks. Mr. Baum, for example, was a person whom you could never ask, "How are you?" for the response always consisted of a detailed recitation of his illnesses, which ranged from an infected liver to a mosquito bite on his toe, all of which he could describe in great detail and with obvious relish. I never knew him to miss a single Sabbath, however, on account of illness. Then there was Mr. Deutsch, a giant of a man with drooping paunch and a bulbous nose, whose sole pleasure in life seemed to be pinching little children's cheeks until they yelled "Ouch!" I knew nothing about his background, nor did that seem important so long as he continued giving us hard sourballs of all flavors to suck on. He kept them in the velvet bag that was supposed actually to hold his prayer shawl. After we discovered this hiding place, we would invent all sorts of ways to distract him so we could help ourselves to the lemon, cherry, orange, and grape contents of the bag.

The highlight of the morning service was the taking out of the scroll. The cantor would walk to the Ark, stand before it as it was opened by one of the congregants, and sing: "Hear, O Israel, the Lord is our G-d, the Lord is One."

All eyes would be on the cantor as he walked slowly down the steps, followed by the rabbi and the Torah reader. The Torah, protected and beautified by a wine-colored velvet cover, embroidered with gold stitching, was cradled like a baby in the cantor's arms.

I was taught from my earliest days that the Torah was the holiest object in our religion. The Torah must be written upon parchment by a scribe using black ink. If even one letter is missing, that Torah is considered unfit for use. If the Torah was dropped, the entire congregation would have to fast. No Torah fell or was dropped in all the years that we prayed at Glory of Israel Synagogue.

A silver breastplate hung over the front of the Torah, and tall silver crowns with bells that tinkled when the cantor walked were placed upon the scroll's rods. The cantor would lead the procession through the synagogue, pausing briefly every now and then by the rows to allow the congregants to kiss the Torah with their hands or lips. There was a man in the synagogue who had suffered a stroke, which had left him partially paralyzed. The cantor would always walk over to him, allowing him to lean over and just barely kiss the Torah with his lips. All the while the cantor was saying: "Exalt the Lord our G-d and worship at His footstool, for He is holy. Exalt the Lord our G-d and worship at His holy mountain for the Lord our G-d is holy."

After the walk around the synagogue the Torah would be brought up to the platform and laid on a large table, known as the bimah, for the reading. Our synagogue, incidentally, had no one who was officially designated as cantor. Most of the members knew how to lead the services. They had gone to synagogues all their lives. Thus we had not one but twenty-five cantors.

The Pentateuch is divided into five books. In addition to

23

telling the story of the Jews, they also contain 613 laws, which all believing Jews are required to follow. Each of these five books is further divided into smaller portions, and each Sabbath a portion of the Pentateuch is read in the synagogue, with smaller excerpts being read every Monday and Thursday morning. The custom of reading from the Torah on Monday and Thursday dates back over two thousand years to the time of Ezra the Scribe. Mondays and Thursdays were especially important because they were market days and because the courts were in session, and the Torah was read for those who had come in from the outlying areas.

During the course of the reading on the Sabbath a minimum of seven persons are called up to the bimah. It is the gabbai's job to determine who is called. The person who receives this honor says the blessing: "Blessed art Thou, O Lord our G-d, King of the Universe, who has chosen us from all the nations and has given us Thy Law. Blessed art Thou, O Lord, who givest the Law." At this point the baal koreh, he who reads the Hebrew words from the parchment scroll, picks up his silver pointer, the end of which is usually carved into a tiny hand with an outstretched forefinger, and proceeds to read a section of the Torah to the tune of an ancient, lilting, singsong melody. After the reading the person who has been called up recites the following blessing: "Blessed art Thou, O Lord our G-d, King of the Universe, who has given us the Law of truth and has planted everlasting life in our midst. Blessed art Thou, O Lord, who givest the Law."

Then the person who has been called up asks the gabbai that a blessing be said for various members of his family or friends. Usually he makes a contribution to the synagogue, and this is announced by the gabbai. There were, of course, individuals called who could not afford to give anything, but even then the gabbai would say that the man had pledged to give a "present," whose contents were never defined. After the person who had been called up had finished, the gabbai would then call up the next person, and the process would be repeated.

Who was called up? A stranger or guest was virtually certain to be asked, as was a person commemorating a special occasion. Beyond that, the decision was sort of arbitrary, and as a result the gabbai needed to be a diplomat. The main thing was to be sure that everyone was called up at least a few times during the year. Naturally, some people desired this honor more than others, and the gabbai had to sense whose feelings would be most easily hurt by an oversight, unintentional as it might be, and who would not be so easily offended. The gabbai also had to have a good memory. The Sabbath law forbade writing because it was considered work, and since it was a small congregation we did not have the more formal system of putting every member's name in a record book and keeping track of who had been called up when by checking his card in a file.

In addition to giving out the honors, the gabbai followed the baal koreh to make certain that he made no mistakes. Biblical Hebrew is usually read with vowels, but the words on the scroll had no vowels. Thus the baal koreh had to know the pronunciation by heart from having studied a voweled version.

Mr. Groob was our baal koreh. A short bristly mustache, a shiny bald head and a rather determined gait made him resemble a martinet, but this was hardly indicative of the man's character. In truth, he was jolly and easygoing, and when he laughed, which was often, his stomach shook visibly. Most of the congregants wore plain prayer shawls with black or blue stripes against a white background, but Mr. Groob's had a collar embroidered with squares of silver.

Although in reality this was not a symbol of any special status, it did make him seem important to me.

" 'Es,' not 'Ais,' " someone would shout. All the members of our shul had Orthodox backgrounds and were capable of following the reader as he recounted the travels of the Israelites through the desert or how they received the Law at Mount Sinai. Naturally, the baal koreh was the center of attention and all were quiet as he read those accounts of our history. Sometimes if the mistake was a minor one, the baal koreh would ignore the correction and simply continue reading. The congregants might, however, continue shouting, " 'Es,' not 'Ais'!" and if they were loud enough, the baal koreh would be forced to repeat the word. To get the young boys (including his own son) to listen to the reading, the reader would offer (after Shabbos) a dime to anyone who could catch him in a mistake. We gladly accepted his challenge, for a dime was no small amount in those days!

I quickly developed favorites among the weekly readings. For example, the story of Joseph and his brothers. How could his own brothers sell him into slavery? And how could Joseph forgive them for this? Or the crossing of the Red Sea, which set the tone for all the lessons I learned about G-d's capacity to save our people no matter how desperate their situation. Each Passover we would sing about how in every generation since the beginning of time the nations of the world had tried to destroy us. And yet each time G-d would intervene and save us, usually in some miraculous way.

After the Torah was read, the Haftorah was chanted by someone in the congregation. This selection generally corresponded thematically to what was being read from the Torah that week. In 168 B.C.E. Antiochus Epiphanes, King of Syria and Palestine, ordered that anyone caught reading the Torah be put to death. In response, the scribes instituted the reading of a chapter of the Prophets each week to replace the Torah reading. It is said that this is the origin of the Haftorah reading.

After the Haftorah came Mussaf, the Additional Service. Someone from the congregation would lead everyone else, as had been done earlier in the morning. Facing the congregation and holding the Torah aloft in his hands, the chazzan (cantor) would say, as the congregation rose: "Let them praise the name of the Lord, for alone His name is exalted."

Before returning it to the Ark, the cantor walked around the synagogue again, allowing everyone who wanted to kiss the Torah to do so. People fell into line and followed the Torah as if to bid it goodbye, until the next time it was taken out. Then as they stood before the now opened Ark, they sang: "It is the tree of life for those who lay hold of it, and they who uphold it are made happy," referring of course to the Torah. The words were sung slowly, as if to delay the Torah's departure just a bit longer.

After this, Rabbi Levy would deliver a sermon in Yiddish.

My friends and I rarely stayed for these speeches, not because we didn't know Yiddish, but because we preferred to play outside in the hall. We had no organized groups led by an older person, as was the case in most of the larger congregations. Nor did we have a special room for a "Junior" congregation, which is an abbreviated version of the regular service with more active participation by the youngsters, held in a separate room in the congregation's building. Our shul, which could hardly afford its rent, was in no position to pay for these luxuries. For me and my four or five friends whose parents also attended Glory of Israel, this was an advantage, for we were free to do as we pleased whenever our fathers let us out. But even more importantly, when we were not permitted to leave, we sat with our fathers and were therefore part of the main service. In fact, even when we ran around, we were part of the synagogue. The entire synagogue, not just one little room, was our home.

Often, while the cantor repeated prayers that had already been said by the congregation, people would walk around and talk with each other. My father, however, kept a pretty tight rein on Mark and me and did not allow us to leave our seats. I still remember the reassuring feeling I got as I huddled against his shoulder and arm, which was partially covered by his woolen prayer shawl.

After services we would crowd toward the back of the synagogue. Wine and whiskey were already on the table, which had been set by those few women who came to synagogue each week. Everyone waited for Rabbi Levy to make the blessing over the wine. After he finished all would drink a little whiskey from a shot glass along with an egg kichel and a piece of schmaltz herring.

When we emerged from the synagogue to walk home, it was already close to noon. Our pace was leisurely, as my father would walk slowly with some of the men, while I walked and played with my friends. By the time we reached home I was really hungry. My father would not pick up the mail before going upstairs since that would mean he was carrying. Besides, we were not permitted to open mail until evening, since it was forbidden to tear on the Sabbath.

We could not turn on the radio or use money, and the law against carrying made it impossible for us even to purchase a newspaper. Although I suppose we could have had the paper delivered, my father simply did not want to read about the news of the world because he felt it was not spiritually conducive to the holiness and otherworldliness of the Sabbath. In fact, our lack of contact with the outside world on the Sabbath was virtually complete and served to reinforce our sense of isolation from irreligious neighbors around us.

The main dish of the Sabbath day meal was cholent, a combination of meat (usually brisket or flanken) and potatoes or beans. Friday afternoon before the Sabbath began it was placed on the stove in a large aluminum pot, where it simmered until the following noonday meal. It was said that the tastiness of the cholent depended on the angels who watched over it while everyone slept.

After grace my father would dance around the room with my brother and me, singing: "Behold how good and how pleasant it is when brothers dwell together in unity." It was all we could do to keep up with him as we whirled around. After our meal, songs and dancing, everyone took a nap. Silence descended over our household until about 3 or 4 p.m.

I would usually be awakened then by my father's gentle prodding. "Wake up, Willy, I've prepared some cake and tea for you." By this time my father was already looking at the Torah reading for the next week, commenting on it as I drank my tea. He did not have the opportunity to study the Torah during the week. In the Talmud the rabbis had said that the Sabbath and festivals were given to the Jews for the purpose of studying the holy works and that this applied especially to those who did not have the chance to do so at other times. Thus my father spent as much time studying on the Sabbath as he could.

Sometimes on Sabbath afternoons we would visit my maternal grandparents in their apartment on Ninety-ninth Street between West End Avenue and Riverside Drive. It was a large apartment with eight or more rooms, and my cousins and I would often run through them playing hide-

and-go-seek as the afternoon sun sank into the Hudson River and the shadows lengthened across the city.

My parents would be in the dining room with the rest of the family eating sponge cake and honey cake, drinking tea out of glass cups. We rarely paid attention to them except when my grandfather would single out one of us for attention. He used to put me on his lap and sing to me in Yiddish. He had a short white beard, whose bristles tickled me whenever he kissed me, which was quite often. His eyes sparkled when he spoke, little flashes of blue fire, and when he smiled, his entire face lit up. Most of the time he would simply bounce me up and down, commenting sometimes on how I looked like this or that member of my family. Although I could not really relate to him (he spoke no English), the caress of his gnarled hands, his laughter-filled voice and the love in his eyes so reassured me that I was completely at ease in his presence.

My grandmother died when I was very young, but I remember a person with honey-colored hair (it was in fact a wig, for, as did many Orthodox women, she kept her hair covered), and the most sensitive brown-gray eyes I had ever seen, murmuring to me in gentle tones, as she gave me homemade cookies from a round-shaped dark-blue tin. I would sit at the substantial mahogany table in the dining room munching on the cookies and toying with the lace tablecloth.

The entire apartment always seemed mysterious to me. There were great stuffed chairs into which I could climb and lose myself. There were family portraits of small children looking serious and dressed in velvet vests and frilly white shirts. These, I learned, were pictures of my aunts and uncles. The huge crystal fruit bowl with the intricately carved leaves and grapes had been brought over from Belgium. My maternal grandparents had managed to escape before the war and had therefore been able to bring many things with them. And yet my mother's family had also suffered. A photograph of one of my great-uncles hung in the living room. He, too, had died in Hitler's inferno.

The apartment was always dark; the furniture looked ancient, foreign, almost out of place, which was precisely the point, for I always felt out of place in America, almost as though I ought to still be in Europe. It was pure fate that had brought us here, rudely and forcibly uprooted and transplanted onto American soil. In reality we were still over there. Our lives here were only adjustments to the changing fortunes of life. Everything of importance had already occurred in Europe. Our wealth was there, so many from our family had died in Europe, my parents' native language was not English, and our religion seemed antiquated to many American Jews. My grandparents' apartment was concrete evidence that this other world had actually existed and that, although it could not be recreated, it could never be totally destroyed either.

On balmy Sabbath afternoons, we would also go for walks in Riverside Park. All the Orthodox Jews gathered there then, especially around Ninety-seventh Street. While the adults talked, my friends and I played. As I got older, however, my father began sending me to a handsome brownstone on a quiet tree-lined street, to study the Talmud in the afternoon for an hour or two with other boys my age. The members of our group were instructed by a serious-looking individual, whose sense of humor matched his countenance. He would drone on while we fidgeted on the hard wooden seats. In other rooms different groups of boys would learn with other equally humorless young men.

After the learning period, we each received candy and cake and heard stories told by Avram Hecht. We sat, about twenty-five of us, on chairs crowded around a long thin table that was covered with a cheap, white, plastic table-cloth. Avram wore a black hat and a faded blue pinstriped suit two sizes too large for him. A thin coating of fuzz partially covered his face. He was trying to grow a beard, and his efforts gave a roundness to an otherwise sharp and intense set of features.

His eyes burning, his hands cutting swaths of emotion through the air, Avram would spin his tales—tales of rabbis and plain townspeople of the small villages of Eastern Europe, tales of suffering and joy, tales that described life as an endless, moving stream of humanity. One felt that the characters did not live happily ever after, but that their entire lives were a series of crises.

I remember especially the tale of the rabbi who came late for Kol Nidre on Yom Kippur, the holiest holiday of the Jewish year. Dressed in white, the entire congregation was waiting for him, yet he was nowhere to be found. What could have happened to detain him? Had he been attacked by bandits on his way to the synagogue? Was he ill perhaps? But no, that could not be, for his wife was in the synagogue, too, and she also did not know where he was. Finally, someone went to investigate and found the rabbi in a peasant woman's hut, feeding wood that he had chopped for her into the fireplace. She was too ill to do it herself. The rabbi, concerned for her welfare, had decided that this task was of sufficient importance to justify delaying the service. From this we learned the significance of gemilus chasodim, being kind to others. Another variation of the story had the rabbi walking to synagogue and stopping in a house to soothe a crying baby whose mother had left him to go to pray.

These stories made the past beautiful. Others might think of the Orthodox Jew of Eastern Europe as a poor soul living in a dirty hut, surrounded by poverty, disease and the hostility of Gentile neighbors, with no opportunity to improve his lot. Not us. We saw that world as a beautiful place where men and women lived a religious way of life and where they genuinely cared for one another. In the old country everyone was religious and kind (of course, the two went hand in hand). The shtetl was a wonderful place, home of delicious gefilte fish, Chasidic leaders who worked miracles and Jews who had pride and dignity.

And yet I wondered, why was G-d so cruel to his faithful servants? Was the Holocaust what we had been chosen for? To die horrible deaths? To see our families killed? Was this to be our reward? The answer most commonly given then (by the few willing to talk about it) was that as human beings our minds were too small to understand the ways of the Lord and that it was not for us to question but rather to believe. At the age of twelve or thirteen to have raised basic questions of faith would have in effect been a challenge to my entire way of life, indeed to my very being. After all, I prayed every day; I ate only kosher food, carefully examining the ingredients written on every candy bar I bought; I wore a skullcap at all times, even when I slept; and I associated almost exclusively with similar children. Raising doubts would be an act of bad faith, both literally and figuratively. Younger, less cloistered individuals might have encouraged such searching, but the generation of the Holocaust erected secure boundaries to ensure continued adherence to the faith.

This was the most negative aspect of Orthodoxy, and yet it was also its most positive, for who could match the happiness of the true believer, his self-confidence and his sense of purpose? How many people go about their daily lives certain of salvation, convinced that G-d, the supreme Maker of the entire universe, has a special interest in them?

After the study group had ended we would go to a brief Sabbath afternoon service. The Torah was taken out and read from. The portion consisted of the first section of the following week's reading, as if to whet our appetites. Following this we went home and had the third meal of the Sabbath, a simple affair consisting of hard-boiled eggs, tuna fish and salad, with perhaps some cottage cheese. The law required that one have three complete meals on the Sabbath.

In the late spring, summer and early autumn, when the Sabbath day was longer, my father would study the *Sayings of the Fathers* with us. This book, actually a portion of the Talmud, was a collection of aphorisms that imparted essentials of Judaism insofar as ethical values were concerned. Each week we would study one of the six chapters, until all were completed. At that point we would start over again. The sayings conveyed basic points of ethical behavior with simplicity and clarity: "Who is rich? He who is happy with his lot." Or: "Be a tail of lions, not a head of foxes." My father's voice was soft and vibrant, filled with love. Mental images of wise men with white, flowing beards, seated in beautiful gardens, discussing the Talmud danced in front of my eyes. "If you follow these sayings, then you will be a happy person," said my father. Whatever doubts I may have had about the accuracy of this assertion were quickly dispelled by the contentment and joy in his face.

We studied until the Sabbath ended, which was about an hour after sundown. Our guideline, whenever possible, was the sky. If one could see three stars, it meant that the Sabbath had ended. Imagine, the Lord had given us a special signal by which to end the holiday—those stars appearing in the sky were actually beaming a message to earth: "Sabbath is over, and the work of the week may begin." We said a few short evening prayers before concluding with Havdalah. Havdalah literally means to "make a separation," and in this case it was the prayer that marked the dividing line between the Sabbath and the rest of the week, between the sacred and the secular. Though short, it was replete with religious significance.

My father filled a silver goblet of wine to the brim, allowing it to overflow as a sign of blessing. My mother in the meantime was lighting the Havdalah candle, as it was called. Essentially, it was a plaited candle that had two or more wicks, which gave it a torchlike appearance. Ours was blue and white. As the youngest, the honor of holding it while the prayer was being recited was customarily given to me. There was also a silver box with tiny holes in it that contained a mixture of spices. It was a beautifully designed box, long and slender with intricate shapes of lions and foxes etched on it. On top was an Israeli flag, whose wavy shape made it appear as though it were blowing in the wind. The reason for the spices was their sweet smell, which refreshed the soul, thus making up in some small way for the "additional soul" that leaves at the end of Sabbath. The lit candle had a religious significance, too. Since creating light on the Sabbath was forbidden, it was considered fitting that the first light used after the Sabbath was over should be for a religious function. In addition, the light reminded the Jews of the first act of creation—G-d's command, "Let there be light."

My father raised the cup of wine in his right hand and the spice box in his left and began the service. I stood near him, holding the candle as high as possible. When he came to the phrase "The Jews had light and happiness, joy and dignity," we all repeated it after him. Each step in the ritual had a special blessing. Thus for wine my father would say, "Blessed art Thou, Lord our G-d, King of the Universe, who creates the fruit of the vine," and following this, "Blessed art Thou, Lord our G-d, King of the Universe, who creates various kinds of spices." At this point, the spice box would be passed around so everyone could smell it. Perhaps it was because it happened only once a week, but I loved the aroma of cloves and held on to the box until prodded by my father's "Nu, nu." (You were never allowed to speak in the midst of a blessing or prayer.) Then my father would say: "Blessed art Thou, Lord our G-d, King of the Universe, who creates the light of the fire." The unsteady light cast by the candle made the room look as though it were bobbing back and forth. We all held our hands up to the flame, letting its light fall upon them.

Then, picking up the cup of wine again, my father intoned the following prayer: "Blessed art Thou, Lord our G-d, King of the Universe, who makes a distinction between the sacred and the profane, light and darkness, Israel and other peoples, the seventh day and the six days of labor. Blessed art Thou, Lord, who makes a distinction between the sacred and the profane." At that point, sitting down, still holding on to the cup, my father would pour some of the wine into a small glass bowl, in which he placed the Havdalah candle, thus extinguishing the flame. "Gut woch!" or "Good week!" everyone would exclaim.

The beauty of such ceremonies has never left me. Everything was so well defined. For every occasion there was a prayer, a ritual. One never walked alone, but always in G-d's presence. He was always with us. I often felt anxiety about G-d. Was this or that omission a sin? Was I doing things the way G-d wanted them done? On the other hand, our ceremonies and laws relieved my guilt by giving me opportunities to demonstrate my love for G-d.

Reluctant to let the beauty of the Sabbath slip away into the night, we often sang songs after Havdalah. One of the songs concerned Elijah the Prophet and expressed the hope that, along with the Messiah, son of David, he would come soon to redeem the Jewish people. According to the Midrash, Elijah entered Paradise every Saturday night, where, sitting under the Tree of Life, he would make a record of who had kept the Sabbath and who had not. According to the Shulchan Aruch (Code of Jewish Law), we did not pray for his coming on the Sabbath because it was not certain if the Sabbath limit upon traveling applied to him wherever he might be. Nor did we expect him to disturb our preparations for the Sabbath by arriving on Friday. Perhaps the most moving of all these opinions was the belief that if all the Jews in the world would simply observe two Sabbaths in a row, the Messiah would immediately redeem us. Imagine, only two Sabbaths! From my perspective as a person who observed every Sabbath, this did not appear to be asking too much.

Succoth, or Booths

(Tabernacles), refers to the temporary huts used by the Israelites during the forty years in which they wandered through the desert after redemption from Egypt. The purpose of Succoth was to recall how the Israelites had lived in a time when they were entirely dependent upon G-d. The period in which it was observed was the end of the harvest season, a time of thanksgiving. This was stated clearly in Leviticus 23:41–43:

And ye shall keep it a feast unto the Lord seven days in the year; it is a statute forever in your generations; ye shall keep it in the seventh month. Ye shall dwell in booths seven days; all that are home-born in Israel shall dwell in booths; that your generations may know that I made the children of Israel to dwell in booths when I brought them out of the land of Egypt: I am the Lord your G-d.

Immediately after the conclusion of Yom Kippur (the Day of Atonement), the holiday that preceded Succoth by five days, my father would join the other Orthodox Jews in the house to build the succah in one of the back courtyards of the apartment building. We obtained planks of wood from a lumber yard and set to work with hammer and nails. Eight or nine men and teenagers were charged with this responsibility. By law the succah had to have at least three new walls while the fourth could consist of a wall that was already standing. While the amateurish way in which the succah was built certainly gave it the appearance of a temporary structure, what really made it temporary was the ceiling. According to Jewish law, one covered the succah with anything that grew from the ground. Thus one could use branches of trees, bamboo shoots or anything similar. This material, known as sechach, was always put on last after all the walls had been erected.

The effect was total. It seemed to me as though I had entered an oasis of joy amid the dreariness of New York City's tenements. The courtyard in which the succah stood was small and narrow, surrounded on all sides by five- and six-story buildings. To see the stars one looked straight up, almost as though one were peering up an elevator shaft. Even when we were inside the succah, the hard concrete on which we walked reminded us that in a sense we were still temporary lodgers in an alien world.

The hostility of many of our neighbors was sometimes brought home to us by vandals who threw rocks on the succah from nearby rooftops. Sometimes my father, angered, would run after them, and once or twice he caught a few of the boys, who, as it turned out, lived in the neighborhood. It was not deep-rooted anti-Semitism that motivated their actions. Rather, it was the perception that we were different in a way that implied exclusiveness. Because we were not aggressive, we became prime targets for bullies and idlers. Still, I could not help feeling that there was a religious basis for this animosity. Sometimes it made its presence known in the casually tossed insult of "Christ killer" that greeted me as I walked in the streets. Other times it was a torn-off mezuzah, a hastily daubed swastika by the door of the synagogue, or rocks thrown at the nearby Hebrew school's bus as it pulled away carrying students home.

The entire activity that surrounded the building of the succah made Judaism spring alive. The succah became our home for the next seven days. Every meal was eaten there and many hours were spent in it chatting and singing with the neighbors. Because of the rock-throwing incidents, it was not difficult for me to imagine how the Israelites must have felt when they were attacked by the Amalekites in the desert.

The day before Succoth, my father, Mark and I went down to the Lower East Side. We took the D train to the East Broadway station. Throbbing with life, the stores were crowded, mostly with elderly Jews. The sidewalks along the narrow streets had become swirling centers of activity, with people rushing to and fro, busily trying to take care of last-minute errands before the holiday. Each holiday had its specific requirements and, consequently, certain streets, depending upon their wares, were busier than others.

For Succoth, it was East Broadway: "Lulavim, esrogim, aravas! Lowest prices here!" Set up on the sidewalks near the gutter were tables, many of them rickety, upon which were placed boxes of esrogim, or citrons. Next to them lay long palm branches called lulavim, myrtle branches (hadassim) and willow branches (aravas). Every Jew was required to have these four items for the holiday. Moreover, he was obligated to purchase the most beautiful ones he could afford.

Next to these tables stood people of all types. Some were clearly businessmen. They looked and acted like professionals. But these were in the minority. Most were simply average people looking to pick up an extra dollar. There were elderly couples standing next to their tables while their children, in all likelihood yeshiva students, yelled, "Here's a metsiya [bargain]! Look at these esrogim, the best on the street!" Literally hundreds of people crowded around the tables, picking up and examining the items, to see if the myrtle branches had three leaves each and if the willow branches were not dried up. Although many people were not that well versed in the laws regarding these matters, each person acted as though he were a mavin (expert).

Later on, in synagogue, when people would remove the esrog from its small box, a box that was generally partially filled with flax to cushion it against accidental jostling or the like, they would look at each other's esrogim and evaluate them. Each person would try to show what a bargain he had got: "I paid only fourteen dollars for this esrog." "Really, how did you get it so cheap?" "Well, my cousin is friendly with one of the people who delivers them and . . ." Or: "How much do you think this esrog is worth?" The other person, if he was a decent sort, would estimate about ten dollars more than he thought it had cost and all would be happy.

We went from one stand to the next examining the different items, but especially the esrog. At every opportunity my father would show me why this or that item was not according to the law, finally selecting the esrog, lulav and other things that he needed, but not before going through the obligatory haggling about the price.

There was an exotic air about the way in which one could emerge from a subway filled with persons from many different cultures, and enter a public street to shouted words whose meaning was familiar mainly to Orthodox Jews. In another day, all these pious Jews would stand in little wooden houses saying the various blessings and performing the acts that had kept our culture alive for so many thousands of years and that held the key to our future.

In terms of attire and going to synagogue, we prepared for Succoth the way we did for the Sabbath. We showered and shaved in the late afternoon and put on fresh clothing. In the synagogue, the velvet covering that hung over the Ark had been changed to one reserved exclusively for use on the holidays. The prayers differed somewhat from those said on the Sabbath, and so each family brought along machzorim, prayer books, that contained these special services. My father's machzor was a heavy black-bound book with a Yiddish translation on the bottom half of each page. I loved to look at the strange, cabalistic drawings in it. Sometimes, for example, the first letters of the lines of a prayer would be arranged alphabetically. How could a prayer be composed with each letter following in order and still make sense? How brilliant, I thought, must have been those rabbis who had composed it.

In the synagogue, members of the congregation often had guests, usually members of their family. This lent a special air to the atmosphere. Members who were not as observant as our family and who came only on holidays were somewhat confused by the proceedings. It was a reflection of the power that the world in which I lived had over me that I determined the good or bad in people by their religiosity or lack of it. If there were religious people who were evil, I certainly didn't know them. Those that I thought ill of were never, in my mind, placed in the same category with the irreligious. And then there were those festival shulgoers who were observant Jews but who, for one reason or another, went to our synagogue on the holidays rather than the one they usually attended.

After the completion of the service, everyone said, "Gut yontif," the traditional holiday greeting, and left quickly.

By the time we got home, my mother would have everything ready. The problem was to get our dinner down the five flights of stairs into the succah. We had six white enamel pots, each filled with food, fitted one into the other and held by a wooden handle. In addition, other things, such as wine, challah, salad and silverware, needed to be brought downstairs.

Upon entering the succah, each male would say Kiddush, the blessing over wine, with a few special phrases uttered in honor of the holiday. Afterward we all went outside the succah to wash. Since there was no water at hand, we had brought it down, along with a tin cup and a basin in which to catch the water as we spilled it over each hand. As usual, my father washed first, followed by my mother, brother and myself. Each person passed the linen towel to the next when he was done. Then, after reciting the blessing over bread, we each said, "Blessed art Thou, Lord our G-d, King of the Universe, who has sanctified us with His commandments and commanded us to dwell in the succah." Now we could relax; the meal could be eaten in peace and joy.

The sharp autumn air intensified the scent of the pine branches that had been used to cover the succah. Looking through the spaces in our improvised and temporary ceiling, I could see the stars. It reminded me of the overnight hikes I used to go on in summer camp, but of course this was different, very different, for we were here to commemorate a historic event in Jewish history. The Israelites might well have looked at these same stars as they sat in the desert waiting and wondering when G-d would lead them to the Promised Land.

We sat on wooden benches crammed in between the walls and a long table, eating and talking with our neighbors. In between courses we sang songs to honor the festival. The sound of our voices reverberated from wall to wall in the small courtyard. I felt a certain comfort in the fact that around us all was silent. As we sang, "Light is sown for the righteous, and rejoicing for the upright of heart," I felt as though I were throwing out a dare to the people around us: "Yes, I believe in G-d, in His goodness and kindness. Yes, I believe that He gave us the commandments to follow, and yes, I believe in the coming of the Messiah. This is what I stand for and I want everyone to know it."

We stayed up late, especially the first two nights of the holiday, often not going to bed until 1 or 2 A.M. Some people actually slept in the succah as well, since the commandment was to *dwell* in the succah for seven days. Although we did not do that, we spent a good deal of time there, not only eating but talking, reading and, in general, doing many of the things that we ordinarily did in our apartment the rest of the year. In fact, only heavy rain could prevent us from staying in the succah.

It was interesting that G-d had commanded us to build these huts not in the spring, the time when the Jews left Egypt, but rather in the autumn, almost half a year later. According to Rabbi Akiba, one of our greatest Sages, this was because in the spring and summer it was natural for people to build huts for shade and it would therefore not have been evident that this was being done to fulfill G-d's commandments. On the other hand, in the fall most people would go into their houses, where it was warmer and no rain could enter. Thus, if we ate in cold booths, it would be clear that we were doing so because the Lord commanded us to. In any event, even when it rained, my father was reluctant to leave the succah, a victim of the elements, and we usually ended up staying until the succah became really wet.

It never occurred to me to inquire how Rabbi Akiba arrived at this explanation. I had been taught to revere the words of our ancient rabbis almost as if they were G-d's.

The next day we went to the synagogue early in the morning. My father took along not only his machzor but the lulav and esrog we had bought on the Lower East Side. The lulav was kept inside a long brown, quite thin paper bag, and the esrog in a small cardboard box. Usually the major holidays of the year—Succoth, Passover, Shevuoth—occurred during the week and not on the Sabbath. As a result, I became especially conscious of what distinguished me from my neighbors. As we walked to synagogue, others, Jew and Gentile, were hurrying to work, stopping briefly perhaps to purchase a paper. After all, New York City did not stop simply because Jews, Orthodox especially, but also Conservative and Reform, were going to synagogue.

Tall and well built, with broad shoulders, Mr. Gordon cut a commanding figure. Steely blue-gray eyes peered out from behind gold-rimmed glasses. He was blond-haired, with strong facial features and a manner about him that suggested wealth and authority. He sat facing the synagogue, looking out sternly at everyone. Mr. Gordon was almost always the cantor for the morning service on the first day of Succoth. He would walk deliberately toward the place where the cantor stood, seemingly measuring each step. When he got there, he would stand motionless, waiting for absolute silence before beginning in a powerful voice, whose beauty was not in the slightest bit marred by its force:

> Thou art G-d in the strength of Thy power,
> great in the glory of Thy name,
> mighty forever and inspiring in Thine awesomeness,
> the king enthroned upon the lofty heights.

When others sang, I often felt we were trying to reach G-d, but with Mr. Gordon I believed we had succeeded.

After the cantor completed the Amidah, or almost inaudible standing prayer, there would be a brief pause before he began saying the Hallel; at that point everyone in the congregation would take out their lulavim and esrogim. My father removed the esrog from its box gently, as though he were holding a precious stone, and, looking at it lovingly, placed it on the bench. He then pulled out the lulav from the paper bag, being careful not to let the leaves on either side of the lulav fall off or become bent.

These leaves, namely the three myrtle branches and the two willow branches, were attached to each side of the lulav (palm branch) by little straw bands. At the start of the Hallel service, the lulav and the esrog were held together by the congregants in one hand. It was necessary that they be checked continuously to make sure they were kosher. If any of the myrtle branches' leaves had fallen out or dried up, it would be necessary to ask a rabbi what to do—if it were still permissible to use them. While we tried to make certain that we purchased only the freshest branches, it was always possible to make a mistake. Not only that, but sometimes leaves might fall off or be bent simply from the jostling and elbowing that were an inevitable part of the ride back home in the crowded subways. The entire combination of branches was called the lulav because the lulav stood higher than the rest of the leaves and was therefore considered more important.

As the lulav was held in his right hand and the esrog in his left, with the stem on top the way it grew on the tree, my father would say the following benediction: "Blessed art Thou, Lord our G-d, King of the Universe, who has sanctified us with His commandments and commanded us concerning the taking of the lulav." If it was the first day of Succoth, we would all also say the blessing, "Blessed art Thou, Lord our G-d, King of the Universe, who has given us life and sustenance and brought us to this season." In this last blessing we were in effect thanking G-d for having kept us alive so that we could observe this mitzvah. It was said on other holidays, too, whenever certain laws were being carried out for the first time that particular year.

We stood throughout the entire Hallel service, a prayer consisting of Psalms 113–118, sung to a number of beautiful melodies, melodies I had learned in the yeshiva and which I loved. Essentially, these Psalms praised the Lord for all the miracles and good deeds that He had performed on behalf of His people. "Who is like the Lord our G-d," we would sing:

Enthroned in exaltation,
who looks down upon the heavens and the earth,
who raises the poor from the dust,
lifts the needy from the ash-heap.
To seat him with princes,
with the princes of his people.
Who turns the barren woman
into a happy mother of children.
Praise the Lord.

Singing the melody in a loud and clear voice, I felt the spirit of the holiday enter me. I had been raised from the ash heap of worldly thoughts, picked up from the dust and seated with princes.

At one point the cantor would say, "Give thanks to the Lord for He is good. For His mercy endures forever." The congregation repeated this chant and then proceeded to wave the lulav and esrog in all four directions: first east, then south, west and north, and finally, up and down. Waving the lulav in this manner symbolized our acceptance of G-d's rule over the entire earth.

Little that we did lacked a reason or explanation. I had once asked my rabbi in school why we used willow and myrtle branches, instead of oak, spruce or some other type of branch. "Because," the rabbi replied, "each of these selections has a separate meaning. The myrtle has a pleasant smell, but is not especially pretty. The lulav has a beautiful shape, but no smell. The esrog smells nice and looks beautiful, while the willow has an ordinary shape and no smell at all. When we hold these items together, what we are doing is symbolically bringing together all the different experiences that life has to offer and expressing thanks to G-d for having given us the opportunity to share in them."

It was, in fact, a unique experience to watch everyone in synagogue perform this mitzvah. The melody was a haunting one that sounded as though someone were trying to summon the Lord. What one actually saw was thirty or forty men waving palm branches in all directions, all the while giving little shakes of the lulavim as the directions shifted. In order to allow for greater concentration during this important prayer, most of the people pulled their prayer shawls over their heads, thereby shutting out everything.

In ancient times the Jews marched around the altar in the Temple every day during the Festival of Booths. To commemorate this custom a scroll was taken out of the Ark at the end of the service and placed on the bench. Then everyone would take his lulav and esrog, form a procession and walk around the bimah. Holding their prayer books in their free hand, they would chant:

For Thy sake, save, we beseech Thee.
For Thy sake, our Creator, save, we beseech Thee.
For Thy sake, our Redeemer, save, we beseech Thee.
For Thy sake, O Thou who searchest us, save, we beseech Thee.

The smaller children would walk next to their fathers, holding on to the lulav and esrog that were firmly in their father's grasp.

At the conclusion of Hallel, the scrolls were taken out and the portion in Leviticus that discussed the holiday was read. I took special joy in following this reading. There, in black-and-white print, was G-d telling us in no uncertain terms to observe this holiday, to obtain various leaves and fruits and to dwell in booths. It was no fairy tale; it was G-d's word.

After the first two days of the holiday, one was no longer restricted as to traveling, turning on a light, etc. One could go to work, and in general act as though it were a weekday. Yet it was still Succoth, in the sense that every meal—breakfast, lunch and supper—had to be eaten in a succah. In order to fulfill this commandment while away from home, my father and the other Orthodox Jews at his place of work on Forty-seventh Street near Fifth Avenue, built a succah right on the roof of the building. Oh, to be sure, my father could easily have done without lunch, but why miss an opportunity to fulfill a mitzvah?

As for me, I can still remember feeling a special sense of excitement as we took the elevator down early in the morning to eat breakfast. We would hurry inside and switch on the electric light that we had attached to a succah beam. Brushing off the pine needles that had fallen onto the tablecloth overnight, we sat down to eat a breakfast of tuna fish, hard-boiled eggs and farmer cheese, anything that did not have to be eaten hot. We were always in a hurry at this time, my brother and I to get to school and my father to get to work. It was precisely that feeling of being in a rush that made me feel the importance of the holiday, for no matter how rushed we were, we still had to take our food downstairs and eat in the succah. And after my father had finished his coffee, which he had brought down in a thermos bottle, we would say grace, thanking G-d for having given us the food that enabled us to survive.

In general, our religious beliefs took a good deal of time from our lives—forty-five minutes or so for prayer in the morning, an hour if we went to synagogue instead of praying at home, fifteen minutes each for the afternoon and evening services, ten minutes more per meal for saying grace. There was even a prayer that every Jew was required to say after he had used the bathroom to relieve himself:

Blessed art Thou, Lord our G-d, King of the Universe, who in wisdom has formed man, creating within him innumerable channels and passages. In Thy sublimity Thou knowest well that were they torn or obstructed we could not survive and stand before Thee. Blessed art Thou, Lord, who heals all flesh and works miracles.

In short, there was practically no activity that I performed in my daily life that did not require acknowledging G-d and His omnipotence. On holidays like Succoth, however, there were even more laws to follow and carry out. In addition to eating in the succah, there were extra prayers to be said. Blessings were made over the lulav and esrog, and we spent more time in the synagogue.

On the seventh day of Succoth, Hoshanah Rabbah, we all went to synagogue in the morning, and toward the end of the service chanted the "Hoshanoth," or Prayers for Aid. On the previous six days, we had marched around the bimah once every day. On this day, we circled it seven times. We were led by the cantor, who on this day wore a white robe, and after we had finished the various prayers asking for G-d's help, everyone took out his "extra" willow branches. These were in addition to the ones we had already bought and placed alongside the lulav. My father had purchased three bunches of five willow branches each. Mark and I each received one bunch apiece. Although the Day of Atonement was the actual day of forgiveness for all sins, Hoshanah Rabbah represented one final chance for repentance. To symbolize this, we were now going to bang the branches against a wooden bench. At a signal from the rabbi, everyone began beating the willow branches hard until the leaves fell off. The only sound in the synagogue was "Whap! Whap!" as the branches thudded against the wood.

Although by law we were supposed to hit the branches only five times, I couldn't resist doing it a few more. As an

Orthodox Jew, raised by European parents, I had few opportunities for committing violent acts. Violence was considered unfit behavior for a future talmid chachem (rabbinic scholar). And yet I felt just as much frustration as the boys on the block whose background did not inhibit physical aggression. Thus I wanted to make the most of one of the few outlets I had for my frustrations. How ironic that even my outlets were religious ones.

Despite the fact that the branches were beaten almost beyond recognition, it was not considered proper to cast aside anything that had been used to fulfill a religious precept. Yet what was one to do with a bunch of mauled willow branches? The answer was that they were kept until shortly before Passover and then tossed into the furnace where matzohs (unleavened bread) were baked. In this way, we were using an item with which one commandment had been fulfilled to aid in carrying out yet another. In general, once something had been used for a religious purpose, it assumed a holy character of its own. This was most evident in the case of prayer books. Many of them were worn and old, with the pages yellowed and, in some cases, torn off. Frequently, when I opened a prayer book in the synagogue, small pieces of paper with one or two Hebrew words written on them, or even a single letter, would flutter down. My automatic reaction, as was the case with every Orthodox Jew, was to quickly pick up the piece of paper, kiss it and put it back into the siddur, or prayer book. One never threw away even one holy letter that had once been part of a siddur. By putting it back, you were preserving its life.

The eighth and ninth days of the holiday were known as Shemini Atzereth and Simchath Torah, respectively. On Shemini Atzereth we prayed for rain, not in America but in

Israel, that water should be plentiful and that the crops should not fail. Why was it so important to pray for rain in Israel, when we were no longer in Israel, when we were, and had been for thousands of years, an urban people? The reason was that no matter where we were it was incumbent upon us to regard Israel as our primary home, to keep our dreams alive while in exile. Although the Jews were scattered throughout the world, their religious practices unified them in a common goal, to return to the Holy Land, to reclaim and rebuild it. In his daily prayers, the Jew mentioned Israel or Jerusalem at least fifty times. He prayed that Jerusalem would be built up again, that all the Jews of the world would return there, and, of course, that rain would come in its season and ensure a bountiful harvest and adequate water for the population. Indeed, from Shemini Atzereth to the first day of Passover, almost one-half year later, we were required to say three times a day, during the silent Amidah service, the following phrase: "Making the wind to blow and the rain to fall."

Toward the end of the service on that day the Kohanim (priests) would invoke a special prayer. In the days of the Temple it was customary for the Kohanim to bless the population; in modern times this practice was followed by descendants of the Kohanim on festival holidays. This was in keeping with the commandment found in Numbers 6:22: "Thus shall ye bless the children of Israel." For the children in our synagogue, it was a mysterious ceremony.

All those who were descended from the original Kohanim would leave their seats and go to the back of the synagogue, where the Levites would wash their hands, just as had been done in the Temple. The Levites also had priestly functions in the days of the Temple, and this was one of them. Then the Kohanim would return to the synagogue and ascend the

52

steps to the small platform in front of the Holy Ark. In the days of the Temple priests were forbidden to wear shoes in the Temple area. Thus the Kohanim standing on the platform were also shoeless, clad either in socks or in slippers made of straw, cloth or rubber. At first the Kohanim faced the Ark. Then the cantor would summon them, calling out in a loud and clear voice: "Kohanim!" The priests answered, "Thy holy nation as it is said," and began to recite in unison, "Blessed art Thou, Lord our G-d, King of the Universe, who sanctified us with the sanctity of Aaron," and then facing the congregation they concluded, "and commanded us to bless his people Israel with love." By this time everyone in the congregation had risen. The Kohanim had put their prayer shawls over their heads so as not to be distracted. Their arms were outstretched at shoulder height and their fingers were spread out in a special way, as they began to repeat the blessing word for word as it was sung by the cantor. The entire congregation also put their prayer shawls over their heads.

While the real reason for this was to show respect for the priests and to enable us to concentrate on the blessing, I had been taught that it was strictly forbidden to gaze upon the priests during the ceremony and that even blindness, G-d forbid, could result from transgressing this law. For many years I would bury my head inside my father's tallith so that I would not look at the priests even by accident, while they were in the midst of this ancient rite. As I got older I became bolder and would occasionally steal a quick glance. When I discovered that my sight was still intact after these experiences, I had my doubts. Of course, I could never express them to my father or anyone else, for to do so would have required an admission of what I had done and that far I was not prepared to go. The result was that such doubts were repressed. Had there been other such instances, I might have begun to question openly the entire belief system, but this was not the case. Most of our beliefs rested entirely upon faith; even where something in the world contradicted our religion, it was usually explained away as being beyond our understanding.

Who were these so-called "priests" dressed in twentieth-century clothes and filled with twentieth-century ideas, yet uttering prayers thousands of years old? They were ordinary folk, grocery store owners, fluorescent light salesmen, waiters, cab drivers. The sole criterion was whether or not one was descended from those who had performed the Temple rites. Thus one had lawyers, corporation presidents and rabbis, too. But whatever their backgrounds, religious qualifications were most often considered first. True, wealthy persons often received honors in the synagogue, but here the poor could stake their claim, too.

The melody used for the priestly blessing was unique. The mournful tones had a wailing sound, whose notes were so stretched out that I had the feeling of being transported back across the generations to the time when all the Jews stood in the Temple listening to the High Priest lead the prayers. We remembered all our traditions. We had preserved them and we adhered to them. All that remained was for G-d to give us the opportunity to renew the days of old. It was frustrating to listen to the priest perform a blessing in a small shul on the West Side of New York City and know that it had once been said in a magnificent Temple. It was torture to pray three times a day for redemption for Israel and not go there, and it seemed unfair to have learned the exact manner in which the sacrifices were presented in the Temple, this animal for that occasion, another animal for a different occasion, to read about the glory of old and to live in the secular, nonbelieving world of twentieth-century New York.

Everyone in my circle knew that the State of Israel was not the real thing, that as a secular state it had lost an essential part of its beauty. Under a secular government, no Temple could be rebuilt, nor could the Messiah come. At the same time we were not anti-Israel. We did not believe, as did many of the ultra-Orthodox Jews, that it was forbidden to settle in Israel until the Messiah came. We gave money to Israel, supported programs that sent youngsters to study there, and in general were concerned about its future. And yet in our eyes something was missing, a feeling that the resurrection of ancient memories through archaeological digs and the like was incomplete. It might be nice to visit Jerusalem, Beer Sheba, Masada and other historic sites, but it seemed equally pertinent to recall that many of the Jews who had lived in those times were G-d-fearing keepers of the commandments.

All our prayers were said with such thoughts and hopes in mind—that G-d's master plan for the world had not yet been carried out. We were in a state of suspended animation, keeping alive our past so as to ensure our future. Would it have been better, perhaps, to have forgotten all the prayers and ceremonies? With no opportunity of being properly fulfilled, they served only to tantalize us, to promise a future whose coming remained indefinite. Would it have been better had we been obliterated like so many other nations, and forgotten that which, though beautiful, could never be? No! That was blasphemy! Turn my back on everything I had been brought up to believe in? Throw away my history, a past which had been preserved for hundreds and hundreds of years? How could I? And so I believed—believed in G-d, the destiny of our people and everything else.

The Lord bless you and keep you.
The Lord make his countenance shine upon you
and be gracious unto you.
The Lord lift up his countenance toward you
and give you peace.

That was the prayer uttered by the cantor. The voices were muffled because I was enveloped in my father's prayer shawl, but I could hear the cantor say each word in Hebrew and the priests repeat after him: "The Lord" repeated, "bless you" repeated, "and keep you" repeated, and so on. And when, after what seemed like ages but was actually only fifteen minutes, I emerged into the bright light, I felt cleansed and happy. The blessing had been rendered and I had conquered my temptation to look.

Simchath Torah means

literally "Rejoicing of the Torah." On that day we would finish reading the last portion of the Torah, the section in which Moses gives his blessing to the children of Israel shortly before his death in the wilderness, and begin reading the Torah again from the time of Creation. The completion of such a cycle was a most happy occasion, one which Jews all over the world celebrated.

For me this was the most joyous day of the year. I could hardly wait for the festivities to begin in our small yet vibrant synagogue. When we walked in, each child was given a paper flag pasted onto a wooden stick on which were portrayed in bright colors various Jewish themes that dealt with the holiday. I held on tightly to my flag, for I would use it later in the evening.

The service was said rather quickly, although no words were left out, and then came the moment that everyone was waiting for. Mr. Gartner, a wealthy member of the congregation, had purchased the honor of the opening prayer and he now assigned a verse each to various people. The Ark was opened and the congregation rose as one of the congregants intoned: "When the Ark moved forward Moses would say: Arise, O Lord, and may Thine enemies be dispersed and they who hate Thee flee before Thee."

And so began the first hakofoh, with six more to follow. Each time the Torah was given out to seven people. Generally, the oldest received first, and with each succeeding procession the honor was given to younger people. If necessary, more than seven Torahs were used, for it was considered essential that every male, young and old, who was capable of carrying the Torah around should do so. The average scroll was quite heavy and difficult for some of the smaller children to hold on to, and so in its place they were given tiny scrolls about a foot high, made of paper rather than parchment.

The cantor marches around the bimah once, with those holding the scrolls walking slowly behind. Suddenly Rabbi Levy leaps into the center of the synagogue and begins singing, "Be happy! Rejoice on Simchath Torah and thereby give honor to Israel's Torah." At that point the entire congregation forms a circle around the rabbi, who has by this time drawn Mr. Gartner into the circle with him. Eyes blazing, face lit up like a menorah, Rabbi Levy holds the Torah aloft from the bottom, firmly grasping the two rods around which the scroll is turned when read. Gesticulating excitedly to Mr.

Gartner, he motions him forward, and together they begin dancing, each holding his Torah high, each advancing three or four steps so that the two Torahs actually touch each other. "For rich is its reward beyond all treasures," the rabbi says and the gathering joins in. "For richer than jewels and gold. In this our Torah we take pleasure and delight for it is our strength and our light." Four or five people suddenly form a smaller circle around Rabbi Levy, who by this time is just beginning to hit his stride. The circle is enlarged as more people, including myself, join in. Holding hands tightly, we whirl around the room to the music of our own happiness. Faster and faster the room begins to spin, windows merge with wall, and the Ark merges with the wooden benches on the side.

Then suddenly the rabbi breaks through the circle. Like moths attracted to a light, everyone follows him. Those who have Torahs hold on for dear life, as they make their way past the swirling crowd now pushing into the aisles. Rabbi Levy, stamping his feet on the ground as he moves, throws open the flimsy glass door with its wooden frame (it once broke during just such a celebration), and descends the stairs to the first floor and out into the street. We all follow, caught up in the excitement. As Rabbi Levy goes into the street, cars come to a grinding halt, many of the drivers annoyed at such an inconvenience while at the same time mystified as to its meaning. We move onto the sidewalk to continue our celebration. Excitedly waving my flag, I am oblivious to the fact that it is 8 P.M., and that people are home. All I can think about is how our joy on this holiday simply cannot be contained within the four walls of the shul. We need space in which to move, air to breathe, and what better place than out in the open under the stars?

The rabbi challenges all comers to dance at his pace in the

middle of a newly formed circle. Suddenly my uncle hoists me onto his shoulders and jumps into the center. I am still holding on to my flag. Rabbi Levy begins singing, "From the mouth of the Lord; from the mouth of the Lord; that is how the children of Israel shall be blessed." Around and around we go as my uncle grabs hold of the rabbi's Torah. I am staring at Rabbi Levy, amazed that so much energy can be both contained and let loose in one person, when he suddenly thrusts the Torah forward into my face. The crowd cheers as I try to wrap my small arms around its center and then, without warning, Rabbi Levy is gone, dancing off with the Torah into the night. My uncle, his burly arms holding me firmly in his grasp, gently lowers me to the ground. "Go upstairs quickly," he says. "The night has just begun."

After a quick dinner at home, we returned to the synagogue to continue the merrymaking. Bottles of whiskey had been especially bought for the holiday. I was usually given only a small shot glass of wine on the Sabbath, but on this night all considerations of propriety were suspended. Because of the strict code of law to which we were required to adhere throughout the entire year, such nights, when discipline was lax, were important, and I'm sure the adults knew it. The look in Mr. Goldblatt's eyes and the indulgent smile of his twin brother, who with him ran Goldblatt's Five-and-Ten, made you feel that as they gave a schnapps to those children who asked, they were thinking back to their own youth. It was as if they were saying, "Go ahead and drink, put off the pain and trouble that is part of growing up just a little longer if you can."

Even when the congregants had drunk a bit too much, it never expressed itself in violence, although inhibitions were loosened. Thus normally reticent Mr. Mazer would unexpectedly burst into a medley of song, combining tunes whose origins only he must have known, and taciturn Mr. Reiner, who spoke only when approached, would become sociable. Rabbi Levy was affected, too. By nature outgoing, on this evening his spontaneous joy and outpouring of praise to G-d exceeded even his normal behavior. His inner saintliness and his view of the world were so dependent upon G-d's all-pervasive influence that if he perceived that G-d wanted His people to be happy on Simchath Torah, he felt obligated to set an example for the others. His frenzied dancing and singing grew out of a wish to encourage others to let go, to act like children of both life and G-d, and to feel free and easy within a framework of spirituality.

This was also our night for visiting other synagogues. During the year one simply did not go from synagogue to synagogue (there were more than thirty Orthodox ones to choose from within a mile radius). Tonight, however, it was traditional to see how other synagogues celebrated and to meet and socialize with friends who worshiped elsewhere. Of all the places that my brother and I visited, my favorite was the Chasidic synagogue, or shtibl, a few blocks from ours. My father's father had been a devout Chasidic Jew in Poland, a follower of the Tchortkover Rebbe, and my own father had been brought up in a Chasidic environment until, at the age of eighteen, he left eastern Poland to live in Germany.

For me, visiting the Chasidic synagogue was sheer ecstasy. We descended three narrow steps to the ground floor of a four-story brownstone located on a side street between Broadway and West End Avenue. Through the window of the shtibl we could see that it was crowded inside. We pushed open the door and saw a solid wall of people whose backs were turned to us. Everyone was facing front. The bulk of the crowd was made up of observers.

With my father serving as a wedge, we managed to move up toward the front. Before us sat the rebbe, or spiritual leader of the group, a man who had come to America from central Poland after World War II and who had resettled on the West Side with the remnants of his former community and those who had become his followers. His beard was long and gray, his face wrinkled with age and suffering. He was flanked by several younger yet virtually identical versions of himself, and the expression on his face was one of pure joy. The rebbe wore a shtreimel, a round hat ringed with beautiful brown fur. His disciples wore large, plain black hats. And upon what was his gaze transfixed? Upon a group of Chasidim who were dancing so rapidly in a small space that it made my head spin simply to watch them.

The niggun (melody) they were singing required no words, for the depth of feeling in the celebrants was so profound that there was no doubt as to their purpose. "Ai, ai, ai, bom. Bom. Bom. Bom." "Give thanks to the Almighty and honor Him" was what they meant. Their body movements were graceful and coordinated, yet so fast I wondered how they managed to keep their balance. As they swung around they clapped their hands, stopping every now and then to stretch them up and out in an imprecating gesture. The room was filled with rapture and ecstasy. We wanted to jump in, but my father restrained us. This was for members only, his stern glance and admonishing forefinger told us. Unaware that his health did not permit him to, I wondered why the rebbe was not dancing. As I looked around, I saw that the benches and tables were in even worse condition than those in our synagogue. Some of the lights were not working.

The dancing slowed down and stopped momentarily as

more benches and tables were cleared to provide more room for the merry crowd.

A new niggun was begun by the rebbe himself. This time, without any perceptible signal, visitors joined in. A school acquaintance, also visiting, pulled me into the line of dancers. A man behind me put his hands on my shoulders, and I followed suit with the person in front of me. We continued dancing this way for a few minutes until a man who had been standing at the rebbe's side jumped into the center, pulled a large white handkerchief from his pocket and held it out in front of him by two corners. Almost as though it had been prearranged, another man of stocky build and medium height immediately leaped into the center of the group. Pressing one thumb against each temple, he stuck out his two forefingers. Then pantomiming a bull charging in an arena, he rushed at the outstretched handkerchief as the first man, playing bullfighter, waved it in the air. Clapping in unison as they happily surrounded the "bullfighters," the other dancers sang an old song that had been composed by the rebbe's great-grandfather, blessed be his memory. The dance had no religious significance, to my knowledge. It was simply a way of having fun.

It was customary for men and women to sit completely separated from each other in this synagogue. The women were on the second floor observing the dancing figures and bobbing heads through small holes in the wooden floor directly over the dancing area.

After a while my father would remind us, "Remember, you have to get up early tomorrow morning for synagogue," and we would reluctantly leave.

The Chasidim, with their distinctive dress, way of life and fanatical devotion to their rebbe, were unforgettable. Once I asked my father, "How come we're not Chasidim?" "Because we have a different way of life," he replied. "But why? And where is our rebbe?" My father looked at me seriously and said, "Willy, although I respect the rebbes because of the holy lives they lead, my only rebbe is G-d. He is the one who makes all the miracles and he even creates all the rebbes. If you learn all the mitzvoth and follow them, then you will never need a rebbe."

During the daytime on Simchath Torah, the festivities began early. The service itself, while not treated lightly, was carried out somewhat differently. For example, the cantor would use a melody from the Passover holiday or sing part of a prayer that was usually read quietly, changes that were regarded with great amusement on the part of the worshipers. Ordinarily, I would have to sit next to my father during the morning service, but today all restrictions were waived. With my friends, I ran around the synagogue getting into all sorts of mischief. One of our favorite games was to sneak up on two (or more) unsuspecting men, tie the fringes of their prayer shawls together, and feign innocence when, upon discovering their predicament, they attempted to untangle themselves. The hakofoth were held again and there was much dancing, as had been the case at night.

Finally, a temporary halt was called to the celebrating, as the reader of the Torah ascended to the bimah to begin the reading. This was, in a religious sense, the most important part of the holiday, since it was the Torah we were celebrating. To outsiders it might seem strange that we should be so happy about the Torah, since it was the source of so many restrictions that were placed upon us. We were permitted to eat only certain foods; we could not use an automobile or ride any vehicle on the Sabbath and on other holidays; we had to wear tefillin, strange-looking black boxes with thongs (phylacteries) on our heads and arms every morning when we prayed; during eight days of the year we could eat no bread; and so on and so forth. Yet the Torah through its laws had enabled us, during all the years of the exile, to maintain our identity as a people. Without it we would have gone the way of other ancient nations, such as the Assyrians, Phoenicians and Babylonians. The Torah was our portable culture. Moreover, those of us who believed in the Torah's guidelines carried them out with pleasure, convinced that they were fulfilling G-d's every wish, thereby ensuring for themselves a place in the world to come.

Years later when I was a budding rabbinical student at the Gates of Israel Yeshiva, I asked an older student of about twenty-one, who was a heavy smoker, how he felt when he could not smoke the entire Sabbath (since lighting a fire on the Sabbath was forbidden). "It doesn't really bother me at all," he responded. "In fact, I don't even *want* a cigarette on Shabbos except toward the very end when it's almost time to make Havdalah. The holiness of the Sabbath is such that in fulfilling it I feel my physical desires giving in to my spiritual feelings."

The reader called all the boys (meaning males who were under thirteen) up to the bimah. Normally, one could not be called up to say a blessing before the Torah until one had reached the age of thirteen, but on this day even this requirement was waived. The oldest among us made the blessing, and as we stood there, a huge prayer shawl was held by its four corners over our heads. This was no ordinary prayer shawl, for everyone fit underneath with room to spare.

The reader began to read the last portion of the Torah: "And this is the blessing wherewith Moses, the man of G-d, blessed the children of Israel before his death." Everyone craned his neck to look into the parchment scroll from which the reader was chanting, his silver pointer moving swiftly from line to line. The way we were jockeying for a position near the reader, one would have thought that we wanted to see every word, but in reality it was simply the excitement of being up there where only adults stood during the rest of the year.

After finishing the last portion, the reader opened up a second scroll and began reading from the first chapter of Genesis: "In the beginning G-d created the heavens and the earth. Now the earth was unformed and void and darkness was upon the face of the deep; and the spirit of G-d hovered over the face of the waters." "Yes, hovered," I thought, snuggling closer to my friend Yitzchak, "just the way the prayer shawl is hovering over us; G-d will protect us as He has done since the beginning of time, provided, of course, we follow in His path." To prove that this was true, we had been presented with an entire pantheon of heroes: Abraham, to whom it had been promised that we would be a mighty nation; Moses, who had led us through the wilderness; Joshua, who had conquered the land of Canaan; King David the just and King Solomon the wise; Bar Kokhba, who tried to restore our lost glory through a futile yet heroic revolt against the Roman oppressors; and the rabbis of the Palestinian and Babylonian academies, who interpreted and elaborated upon the teachings of the Torah through their writings in the Mishna and Talmud.

The reader would describe all that had been created in six days, concluding with "And G-d blessed the seventh day and hallowed it; because that in it He rested from all His work which G-d in creating it had made." And then, out of nowhere it seemed, we were bombarded. With what? Candies, of course! Pandemonium broke loose. Sourballs, lollipops, Tootsie Rolls and fruit candies were coming at us, mostly from the women's section. We scrambled for them wherever they landed, between people's feet, on benches, window sills, the bimah, and in our hands, if we were lucky enough to catch them.

Once we had enough, we began throwing them ourselves at other people, taking special aim at the cranks (every synagogue had them), who lacked a sense of humor and who were known to have no patience with children. Sometimes we got into trouble with our parents for this, but mostly our behavior was treated with understanding and tolerance.

After services we went home exhausted and ate lunch. Thus the afternoon was spent in a relaxed manner, reading, conversing or taking a short nap. By evening, when the holiday ended, things were more or less back to normal. It would be several months before Chanukah, the next celebration on the Hebrew calendar.

I woke up around 6:30 A.M.,

earlier than usual. The rays of the morning sun were just beginning to filter into my room, which overlooked a small courtyard. Yet it was not the sun that had disturbed my sleep, but rather the fact that it was the first day of school after a summer of fun-filled vacation.

I would again be with my friends, whom I had not seen for almost two and a half months. Would Gary still be angry with me because I didn't invite him to join the last punchball game before school closed for the summer? Had David's parents bought him the new bike he wanted, and if so would he let me ride it? These were, of course, crucial questions for me at the age of nine. Later on I was to leave the world of fun and games for a period of time and totally immerse myself in studying the laws and culture of my people, so that virtually anything else I did would make me feel guilty and ashamed. On this morning, however, these were the things I was thinking about.

I dressed quickly, making certain to say, "Blessed art Thou, Lord our G-d, King of the Universe, who has sanctified us with His commandments and bidden us to wear a fringed garment," as I put on this piece of clothing which lay between my undershirt and shirt and which every Orthodox Jew was required to wear. Actually, I did not have to fulfill any commandments now because I was not yet thirteen, the age at which every Jewish male is considered an adult and thus responsible for all his actions. Yet, since it was considered good training for that day to come, I, and every other Orthodox Jewish friend I had, fulfilled all the commandments as though we were already of age. I might add that the net effect of this was to make us look forward with great eagerness to the day when everything we did really "would count."

The fringed garment was made of lamb's wool and fit over my shoulders. On each of its four corners were eight threads and five knots, also made of wool. These were the fringes, or tzitzis, and if one string was missing, the entire garment was considered unfit. Every Jew was required to wear this garment all day so that, according to Numbers 15:39, ". . . ye may look upon it." The significance of this law was further heightened for me when I learned that the Hebrew letters of the word "tzitzis" (in Hebrew each letter of the alphabet stands for a number) when added together came to

67

a total of 600 and that when this figure was added to the 8 threads and 5 knots, the sum was 613, the number of commandments in the Torah.

For me this was a divine sign from the Lord telling us of the importance He attached to the fulfilling of this commandment. At this point in my life, I wore the tzitzis tucked into my shirt. In later years, however, when I entered the yeshiva, I would display them openly, letting each of the four groups of strings hang out for everyone to see.

"Good morning, Willy," my father said, as I came into the living room. "You'd better hurry up or you'll be late for school." I sat down at the table and opened up my prayer book. Although my father had bought it for me only last year, it was already somewhat worn and dog-eared from constant use, for I prayed from it every morning and evening. I began saying the blessings somewhat hurriedly and was immediately admonished by my father. "Don't rush through the prayers. You can do everything else quickly, but you should always set aside a certain amount of time for G-d, who created you and gave you the capability to do everything that you do."

"Blessed art Thou, O Lord our G-d, King of the Universe, who has given to the rooster intelligence to distinguish between day and night." That was the first of fifteen blessings with which I began the morning service. All the prayers were said aloud in accordance with the Code of Jewish Law, written in the sixteenth century, which stated that this practice improved one's ability to concentrate. The prayers took about forty-five minutes, and when I had finished, breakfast was already on the table, usually in the form of scrambled eggs or a tuna fish sandwich. I ate quickly and rushed off to school.

The Light of Abraham Yeshiva was conveniently located

two blocks from my house. The building, a dark-gray brick structure, was four stories high with tall windows on each floor. In the lobby, about five feet beyond the entrance to the building, was a gaily lettered sign suspended on a long string attached to opposite walls. The Hebrew letters, which had been cut from paper of various colors, spelled out the words "Blessed are those who arrive." The walls were covered with paintings done by students.

As I arrived, the orange and black buses were unloading. Screaming, laughing boys and girls poured out and ran up the stone steps and through the glass doors. Within a week, their fingerprints would make them virtually impossible to see through. We lined up in the gym according to class and then made our way to the second floor. I took a seat near the front, for, as always at the beginning of the school year, I planned to pay attention all the time.

Although of short stature, Mr. Schwartzchild, my new teacher, made a rather formidable impression on me. Perhaps it was his hard, sky-blue eyes set back in a bony, line-creased face. His nose was straight and sharp-angled, and his thin lips looked as though they would have great difficulty parting in a smile. He demanded our absolute attention, and successfully conveyed to us the fact that he meant business.

Naturally, there were students who were not easily intimidated even by Mr. Schwartzchild, but they eventually learned their place. I will never forget the time Mr. Schwartzchild talked with Dr. Heisler, our principal, about Harvey Dachs, a student whose love for spitball-throwing far exceeded his interest in the mechanics of Hebrew grammar. One day, after two warnings had failed to impress Harvey, Mr. Schwartzchild suddenly strode over to a corner of the room, where he picked up a window pole (it was more than twice his size). Returning to the center of the room, he began tapping on the loudspeaker, which was hooked up to the principal's office. Three light taps were followed by a pause, and then, without warning, Mr. Schwartzchild began speaking: "Dr. Heisler, I'm calling you about Harvey Dachs. He doesn't seem to be interested in his studies and I thought you might like to know."

We all sat dumfounded, staring at the loudspeaker. We had heard announcements over it, but no one had ever spoken to it. Mr. Schwartzchild appeared to be listening intently now. He cupped his hand over his ear, asking "What?" and saying "I see" between pauses. We heard nothing, and yet I felt apprehensive. Finally, Mr. Schwartzchild said, "So you think I should give Harvey one more chance, but only if he promises to behave." Another short pause, and then: "Okay, if he causes any more trouble, I'll get in touch with you."

Mr. Schwartzchild put the window pole back in its place, turned to the now ashen-faced Harvey and said: "We will now continue with the lesson."

That was the year we learned the fascinating story of the Israelites' enslavement in Egypt and of the Ten Plagues that G-d brought upon the Egyptians to break their will and thus force them to let our people go. We read these stories as they appeared in the Bible in the original Hebrew, the very same tongue in which G-d had spoken when He commanded Moses to demand the release of his people from Pharaoh. And so through the power of language I was transported back to the time of the Israelites and made to feel at one with both G-d and my people. After all, I, too, would have been a slave in Egypt had I been alive then.

To us the Bible was not simply a nice folk tale. It was a factual, historical account of our people, one that needed to be carefully learned, absorbed and remembered.

Starting in the fifth grade, we began studying the more difficult portions of the Pentateuch, namely the laws of the religion—the laws that had formed the basis for the conduct of the great Biblical figures, such as Moses, Aaron, Joshua and the others. Needless to say, we were all aware that whatever happened to the Israelites was dependent upon their following the commandments. The faith required to do so did not seem difficult once one accepted the validity of the Torah, for it seemed a rather straightforward affair. Those who believed in G-d were rewarded; those who did not were punished.

I came to perceive the idea of believing in that which could not be seen as a true test of my faith. This was brought home to me by the following legend about the giving of the Torah: The Lord went to various nations and offered each of them the opportunity to receive the Torah, explaining that acceptance of it would mean that they were required to obey all the commandments. Each nation asked G-d to describe to them the contents of the Torah before they would commit themselves. The Israelites, however, said: "We will do and then we will listen." For this act of faith, they were rewarded with the chance to fulfill G-d's wishes to the fullest extent possible. The point was not lost upon me. If I believed without questioning, I, too, would be blessed and rewarded by the Lord.

Immediately above the blackboard was a rolled-up document which, when unfurled, depicted the land of Israel as it had appeared in Biblical times. We were required to memorize the names of the places through which the Israelites passed during their forty years of wandering through the desert. We knew that the Patriarchs and their wives were buried in Hebron; that Sodom, the city destroyed by G-d

71

because of its wickedness, was located in the southern portion of the country; and that the ancient city of Shechem (Nablus) was situated north of Jerusalem. The map was a detailed one, showing by color scheme and design where the mountains lay and where the fertile areas were to be found. Looking at the hills surrounding Jerusalem, the Red Sea and the Sinai Desert, I felt conscious of the past moving closer to the present, the ancient merging with the modern, and myself drawing nearer to everything that I believed in.

In the back of each classroom was a long wooden shelf filled with softcover Hebrew books. Written in simple Hebrew prose with many of the key words translated into English, they spanned the entire range of the Jewish experience. There was the story of Eldad haDani, the ninth-century traveler who claimed to have come from the lost tribe of Dan. Now there was a tale worth knowing. In 722 B.C.E. the Assyrians had conquered the kingdom of Israel and had scattered its inhabitants throughout their farflung empire. As a result, ten of the twelve tribes were lost forever. Forever, that is, until the report of Eldad haDani, the famed Jewish traveler.

According to him, many Israelites, especially from the tribe of Dan, still lived in a remote part of the world. Access to their land might be gained only by crossing the Sambatyon River, a wild body of water that hurled forth large boulders and rocks every day of the week except on the Sabbath, when, like the G-d who created it, it was at peace with itself and with the world. Apparently, the river became actually passable for only a few minutes before the beginning of the Sabbath, and it was during this brief period that Eldad had crossed it.

Oh, how I wished that I could have been there! To have looked upon the face of my brother whose tribe had lost

72

contact with the Jewish people for so many centuries and to have spoken with him. Never for a moment did I doubt the authenticity of these events. As I looked at the drawing of the elegant dark-bearded Eldad haDani on the green cover of the book, sitting majestically astride his beautiful white horse, I felt a close kinship in the knowledge that he was mine and mine only—a conviction probably shared by many of the other boys and girls in my class.

G-d knows, we needed our heroes. The drawings in some of the other books of Russian-Jewish children cowering behind their mother's bed as the Czar's agents came to carry them off to fight in the army for periods of up to twenty-five years were embedded in my memory. Yet heroes emerged even during the dark, sad days of Jewish history when calamity after calamity befell our people. For instance, there was Hannah Senesh, who parachuted into Yugoslavia during World War II, and then made her way to Hungary to fight with the partisans. Tragically, she was captured and executed by the Nazis. She refused to reveal the secret code of the underground despite brutal torture. Most important perhaps, she had willingly left the then relative safety of the land of Palestine to fight on behalf of her people.

I cherished the hour or two a week that we spent reading those books. I can well remember the many hours pleasantly lost in the pathways of history.

The wonders and delights of the Jewish Museum on Fifth Avenue, as well as the intricacies of the Horowitz-Margareten matzoh factory, were also revealed to me in those years.

Naturally, there were trips to places of general interest, too, for we were, by contemporary Orthodox standards, a modern institution. We took trips to the New York Times Building, the Museum of Natural History and the Hayden

Planetarium. This concern for teaching us about the larger world was most apparent in the importance placed upon secular, or "English," studies, as they were referred to. We had science labs, an annual science fair, an excellent library and a highly qualified faculty. Hebrew classes were held during the morning hours and the English subjects were given in the afternoon. As a result of this "double schedule," the school day was a long one compared to public school. By the time I reached the seventh grade, I was in school until five o'clock.

Although the secular and the religious were blended together in such a way that, in terms of doing well, I never thought of one as being more important than the other, the fact was that the subjects were being taught in a yeshiva. When we drank milk from a container, we were required to say the appropriate blessing. There was a mezuzah at the entrance to each room in the school, and we always wore our skullcaps.

Every morning when we entered class, the teacher would appoint a student to lead us in prayer. The classroom was decorated with flowers and drawings created by the children. I remember how Mrs. Freilich, our second-grade teacher, would call upon pupils to recite various stanzas and we would eagerly anticipate our opportunity to show off. The lines at the corners of her eyes would become distinct whenever she smiled, which in her case occurred quite often, for she was a happy woman. Her steel-gray hair was frizzy and shaped like an Afro, giving her face a round and jovial expression. A pair of rimless spectacles sat shakily on the bridge of her nose and sometimes, when she became especially excited, they would fall to the floor.

The school choir was one of the more memorable extracurricular activities in which we engaged, at least those of us who could carry a tune. I loved the time spent in the large room on the fourth floor. We all sat on gray-painted metal folding chairs, the altos on one side of the room, the sopranos on the other.

To be in the school choir meant not only that there were special times when one could be excused from regular classes for practice, but also that we might sing at places outside the school. For example, on Chanukah the choir often sang on NBC's Channel 4. One boy would light the Chanukah candles and sing the blessings. The rest of us stood behind him singing for all we were worth, fully aware that this was a most special event. The camera would swing across the studio, pausing first on this child, then on that one, perhaps even on me. Everyone stood tall and straight, hoping to be captured and recognized for the eternity of ten public seconds. I, like all the others, wore dark-blue trousers, starched white shirt, dark tie and a white skullcap. We were on TV, and the world, or at least our world, was watching. Afterward everyone would tell us how *fabulous* our performance was and how *adorable* we looked.

Every day after Hebrew classes were over, we lined up and trooped down the stairs to the lunchroom, where we were served a good wholesome meal by Mr. Mirowitz, a portly and kindly-looking man with a ruddy complexion and large ears, whose black yarmulke was always perched so precariously on his head that it looked as if his slightest movement would cause it to fall off.

In addition to serving in his regular position, Mr. Mirowitz gave a cooking class for the girls. It was he who introduced us to pizza. In compliance with the law that we could eat only properly slaughtered meat and eat no pork, shrimp or other food proscribed by the Torah, we were required to consider the ingredients in every food product purchased.

For example, we could buy only bread or cake made from pure vegetable shortening. In the case of pizza, we were unable to eat the cheese because in many instances it contained nonkosher enzymes. In the 1950s there were no kosher pizza shops, and so Mr. Mirowitz's version of pizza made in a square shape became the definitive one for me.

At the end of the meal we would sing the grace, one student leading the entire school. Holding the microphone near him, he would begin: "Let us say grace," and three hundred-odd voices would immediately respond: "Blessed be the name of the Lord from time forth and forever." Then, continuing, he would intone, "With the sanction of those present we will bless Him of whose bounty we have partaken," and back would come the answer loud and clear: "Blessed be He of whose bounty we have partaken and through whose goodness we live." Then the fun began. Every blessing within this prayer had a special melody. Some were fast and snappy, while others had slower-measured tempos. Frequently, we would make up new endings to some of the melodies, and our teachers, although they took the blessings very seriously, would indulge these deviations provided they were not too radical, for after all, we were children.

We thank Thee, O Lord our G-d, because Thou did give us a heritage unto our fathers, desirable, good and bounteous land. And because Thou did bring us forth, O Lord our G-d, out of the land of Egypt and did redeem us from the house of bondage. . . . Thy covenant which Thou has sealed in our flesh, Thy Law which Thou has taught us, Thy statutes which Thou has made known unto us, the life, grace, and loving-kindness which Thou has presented to us, and for the food that Thou does feed and sustain us on every day, in every season and in every hour.

Needless to say, I did not think of G-d every time I looked at food, nor even every time I took a bite from a sandwich, or drank a glass of milk, and yet I said blessings so often before eating that it literally became a part of my being. Whenever I looked at a fruit or vegetable, I would mentally note the proper blessing. All this served to make G-d nearer and dearer to me. I could talk with Him, and if that was true, then He must be listening to me.

On Friday, a student who had a particularly good voice would lead us all in songs for the Sabbath, the same ones that I sang with my parents on the holy Sabbath itself. Yet, despite the fact that I would be reciting them at home that very evening and on the following day at the Sabbath lunch meal, it was important that they were sung in school, for it made the ties that I had to my religion and culture even stronger. Here were melodies that I and my family sang in the privacy of our home being repeated in the public forum of the school.

Invariably, we had the best meal of the week on Friday. When the Israelites were wandering in the desert, G-d sustained them by sending down manna from heaven, a remarkable food which tasted like whatever one wanted it to taste, from chicken to grapes, from ice cream to steak. Friday, however, was special, for G-d sent down a double portion of food, one for Friday and the other for the Sabbath, since, after all, G-d rested on the Sabbath, too. How receptive our imaginations, with their yearning for the seemingly unattainable, were to such descriptions of the miracles witnessed by our forefathers.

Though most of our holidays were observed in both the home and synagogue, a few found their expression primarily in school. One of these was Tu Beshvat, which translated into English means the fifteenth day of Shevat, one of the Hebrew months. This day was the New Year for trees. It had originally been mentioned in the Mishna, a code of Judaic Law edited and published about 200 C.E. In school our teacher gave each of us a small paper bag containing different fruits and candies to commemorate the festival. Whatever the bag's contents, it was certain to include a fruit from a tree that grew in Israel, most often a bokser (St. John's bread) from a carob tree. In addition, we sang songs about the blossoming of the trees and how the sun was helping them grow. The classroom itself was invariably decorated with flowers and leaves.

Why all this fuss about trees? First, we were taught to respect all things that G-d created, and second this was just another way of bringing us closer to the Holy Land. In Israel it was customary for children to celebrate the holiday by going on field trips, but in New York this was both impossible and irrelevant, for Tu Beshvat always came around January, the middle of winter. The fact that we were talking and singing about a feature of spring while outside it was freezing heightened my sense of isolation from the non-Jewish world around me while at the same time drawing me closer to my religious environment.

This sense of conflict between the outside world and my own community was an important feature of my life. I realized at an early age that Jews had good reason to rejoice when our enemies were destroyed by G-d and that we did have a glorious history. At the same time, there was a tension in being Jewish. The furtive glance at the Gentile boy across the street sitting on the stoop. Would he yell "Christ killer" at me or might he mercifully continue talking to his friend and thus fail to notice me slipping by with my briefcase on my way home from school? I had been beaten up by anti-Semites in my neighborhood, and members of my family had been killed in Europe for being Jewish.

For a people with so much going for us, we seemed rather unsuccessful and quite timorous. The only constant was the intensity of our feeling. Whether it was joy or sadness, Jews tended to emphasize the human quality of these emotions. Many of us wept on the day that marked the destruction of the Temple, just as tears of joy expressed our happiness on Simchath Torah. In sum, religion itself held us together. It comforted us, scolded us, told us what to do and held out the promise of reward—not in some distant place in the sky, but in the deep satisfaction that came from living the life of a devout Jew. This was our compensation for our suffering, suffering that I came to believe was due to the jealousy of our neighbors at the richness and fullness of our lives.

While the lack of social contact with Gentiles that characterized our daily lives probably contributed to the way in which I and my friends and relatives perceived the world, I have no doubt that such an attitude had been an absolute necessity for us to have survived the hostility and violence of so many centuries.

Perhaps the central figure during my years at the Light of Abraham School was the principal, Dr. Heisler. If Mr. Schwartzchild was intimidating, Dr. Heisler was frightening. Mr. Schwartzchild commanded our respect, but Dr. Heisler we held in awe. A pair of deep-set black eyes glowered from behind dark-rimmed glasses, whose unusually thick lenses made them loom quite large. His dress was impeccable and tended toward pinstriped suits with solid-colored dark ties, starched white shirts and shoes that were always shined. His thin black hair was neatly combed straight back. But it was his voice that was most unforgettable. On one occasion it would be low yet menacing, and on another soft in a way that encouraged you to confide in him, to perhaps tell him who had put the thumbtack on the teacher's chair. In the lunchroom he would be loud and cheerful as he drove us to sing the grace with more feeling and devotion; yet in the hall that same loud voice became a powerful hint of punishment to come should you be caught without a pass from the teacher. His deliberate walk, like that of a cat stalking a mouse, was itself sufficient cause for alarm. And you didn't run when Dr. Heisler spotted you. He knew everyone in the school by name.

Sometimes we received prior notice of his coming. We might be running around the room because of an absent teacher, when suddenly one of the students would come in from the hall, yelling, "Quick! Manny's coming!" Naturally, when he walked in, all were in their seats, sitting at attention, hands folded in front of them. Dr. Heisler would seem not to notice that at least half of us were still panting and that others were visibly perspiring. He would begin by announcing the name of the substitute who would take the place of the regular teacher that day and end by warning us to be on our best behavior, a warning no one took seriously, for substitutes were fair game for our antics.

In terms of discipline, he always seemed to be one step ahead of us. He had a way, either through conspiratorial cajoling or by bullying threats, of discovering the truth in almost every situation. On one occasion we had all been given little circular calendars made of two pieces of cardboard, one behind the other. As one moved the cardboard, different dates of religious significance would appear in a little cut-out space that formed a tiny window. Our interest in the dates lasted only until we discovered that these devices made excellent flying objects. What fun we had then as we tossed them around to each other! It took only two minutes for the room to be full of cardboard flying saucers whose owners made merry oblivious to the shouting of the teacher, one of the more hapless in the school.

Then, unexpectedly, the door opened and in walked Dr. Heisler, who demanded to know what was going on, while we tried to retrieve our calendars. He asked that those who had been throwing the calendars come forward. No one moved. Picking up a calendar that lay at his feet, Dr. Heisler asked whose it was. No one said anything. Glaring at everyone in the room, Dr. Heisler said: "Will everyone please hold up their calendar?" Almost before we grasped the intent of his request, the whole class held them up high in the air. That is, with the exception of Jamie Sitkin. "Is this yours?" asked Dr. Heisler, in a voice dripping with sarcasm. Then, without waiting for a response from our now terror-stricken classmate, he said: "Come with me down to my office, Jamie." The result was a two-day suspension from school, coupled with a brief visit to the principal's office by Jamie's mother.

Naturally, it was forbidden to play with baseball cards while classes were in session, and when I was caught one day for the second time in a period of four hours flipping them off the wall, Dr. Heisler not only confiscated them but also marched me down to his office. There I received a good scolding and was told, "Even though you're a good student, I'm sending for your father, because if I don't, you will no longer be a good student."

In the sixth grade, I was exposed to the world of the Talmud, a sixty-three-volume work of immense complexity, written in the Aramaic language, a tongue spoken thousands of years ago in Mesopotamia but long since dead—

dead, that is, with the exception of the Talmud, where the ancient laws and beliefs of the Jewish religion are interpreted and discussed. Though written almost fifteen hundred years ago, the Talmud's teachings are still considered valid today by Orthodox Jews. Among the topics it covers are marriage, caring for the sick and aged, science, mathematics, government, criminal law, charity and virtually anything that can possibly occur in one's daily life.

I was a child of eleven and the legalistic maneuverings of the rabbis as they parried intellectually with one another struck me initially as quite confusing. One thing was clear, however. A battle of wits was going on. While it was almost a year before I began to feel confident in my grasp of the Talmud's approach, I learned much earlier that the Jewish way was to fight with words—that if one could achieve one's point verbally, the battle was won. It became clearer each passing day that what was respected in our world was knowledge and understanding.

Many times a segment in our Talmudic studies concluded with one rabbi admitting to the other that his position was in error. It was as though a game of sport had been played and one participant had emerged victorious. Only, it was not a game. It was our heritage, our way of life, that was being analyzed and debated. So much of what we learned had direct applicability to our daily lives. And even where it did not, as in the discussion of what type of sacrifice to bring to our no longer existing Temple, it had potential relevance, for one day the Temple would surely be rebuilt. In but a few short years, the study of the Talmud would become the very essence of my existence, a clear manifestation of my determination to escape the limitations of earthly desires and cravings by entering into a totally harmonious relationship with my Maker. At the moment that day was still far off.

And yet if I had known what lay ahead of me, I would have realized how each hesitant step that I took in those early years was setting me ever more firmly and irrevocably on the holy path in my quest for true faith and happiness.

By the time I reached the eighth grade, I had already demonstrated considerable aptitude in Talmudic studies. As always, my father tried to help me improve myself. Upon learning that we were studying a particular portion of the Talmud, he immediately made a trip down to the Lower East Side, where he purchased a book of commentaries on the section I was studying in class. Not that my rabbi was failing in his efforts to explain the material. It was simply that my father wanted to help me excel in this most important subject and felt that he could best do so by understanding the material himself as thoroughly as possible.

By evening, after supper, my father and I were both tired, he from a full day's work and I from a whole day of school. And yet we reviewed the material I had learned that day. At first it was brutal. In the sixth grade we studied the Talmud —or Gemara, as we called it—only three times a week for thirty-five minutes a session, and I found the concepts difficult. (Actually, the Gemara is but one portion of the Talmud. Basically, the Talmud consists of two sections—the Mishna, which is primarily the interpretation of Biblical law, and the Gemara, which consists of commentaries on the Mishna by later scholars. Nevertheless, it is customary among Orthodox Jews to use the terms "Gemara" and "Talmud" interchangeably.) There were times when my father would have to review a certain point four or five times before I could comprehend it. At other times I was simply unable to fathom the argument altogether. The language was so foreign, and the type of reasoning used so alien to my ordinary way of thinking. Moreover, each point was built upon the previous one, which meant that one had to remember all the preceding arguments before going further. Frequently a point would be substantiated by a reference to another portion of the Talmud, and it would then become necessary to familiarize myself with that discussion as well.

On more than a few occasions I burst into tears, tears of frustration and anguish at my inability to understand what was being said. My father, always patient, would put his arm around my heaving shoulders and say, "Don't worry, you'll get it. Why don't you try it once more? You'll see. You can do it. You just have to want to." And although I was bitter, abject and skeptical, I would make the effort once again, if for no other reason than the fact that he still believed in me.

My father was correct. My perseverance paid off and I learned yet another quality: determination. I could do it; I *would* do it. Most importantly perhaps, the joy I felt when, in a flash of light, I understood what the rabbis were saying easily made up for my suffering. The adrenalin would surge through every last fiber of my body. As the Talmud said: "I had sought and I had found!"

"He will learn quickly enough. He has a good ear." The voice belonged to Rabbi Yechezkel Samet. I was then twelve years old, with less than a year to go before the day when I would assume the responsibilities incumbent upon every Jewish adult male—fulfilling G-d's commandments.

Rabbi Samet began by teaching me the melody traditionally used for the weekly portion of the Torah that would be read from the scroll, for on my Bar Mitzvah day I would take over that duty from the reader, or baal koreh. In addition, he taught me how to lead the congregants in the service. Actually, I had already learned the melodies used by the cantor simply from having attended services regularly. Finally, I was given a speech to memorize. The topic dealt with tefillin or phylacteries. These were the two little black boxes inside of which were written four Biblical passages, the purpose of which was to remind the Jew of his obligation to follow in the path of the Torah. Located in different portions of the Bible, each passage dealt with the commandment to put on tefillin as a sign of Jewish belief and devotion. Attached to the boxes were leather straps which, like the parchment and the boxes themselves, were made from kosher animals.

Every morning, at prayer time, a Jew was required to don these boxes, one on his head, the other on his arm, tied with straps and kept on until he had finished praying.

More than anything else, tefillin was the mitzvah that made me feel the significance of my newly acquired status. It was the most tangible evidence that I was now a man. I can vividly recall the excitement that gripped me when I acquired my first pair of tefillin. They were in a blue-velvet bag. In the center was a gold embroidered Star of David set around the word "tefillin." On top, also stitched in gold, was my name in Hebrew: "Naftoli Helmreich" (Naftoli was the name of one of Jacob's twelve sons). Actually, I put on the tefillin for the first time on the weekday of my thirteenth birthday. One does not wear or even touch tefillin on the Sabbath, for the Sabbath alone is a more than adequate reminder of G-d and the use of yet another symbol of that awareness was considered unnecessary.

In preparation for my Bar Mitzvah, over a period of about six months, I learned the Torah reading, the Haftorah and my speech, which was to be delivered in Hebrew and in English. In addition, my father and I practiced the service, for I was also to be the cantor on that day. I wanted to do a good job in front of my classmates, who were coming to our synagogue that morning. Similarly, my parents looked forward to it as an opportunity to demonstrate to friends, relatives and members of the congregation what *their* son could do. My parents had taken me to Gimbels department store and fitted me for a navy-blue suit. This, along with a solid-blue tie, gold tie clip, a light-blue fedora hat and a starched white shirt, was to be my uniform.

Fortunately, the day went off without a hitch. I carried out my duties well enough to win the approval of even the most critical experts in the congregation. I derived the most satisfaction from chanting the beautiful melody of the Haftorah, for its theme that day was a most pressing one. It was the Sabbath that occurred between Rosh Hashonah (the Jewish New Year) and Yom Kippur (the Day of Atonement). As such it was given the name "Sabbath of Return," referring, of course, to the idea that the Jews should repent for their sins now that the Day of Judgment was so near at hand. The Haftorah reading reflected this concern, beginning with the passage taken from the Book of Hosea: "Return, O Israel, unto the Lord thy G-d, for thou hast stumbled in thine iniquity" (Hosea 14:1). The reading of those words stirred the depths of my soul, for the exhortations to repent were, as always, followed by a description of the rewards that awaited those who believed and followed:

I will be as the dew unto Israel.
He shall blossom as the lily
and cast forth his roots as Lebanon.

His branches shall spread.
And his beauty shall be as the olive tree.
And his fragrance as Lebanon.

Although there was a kiddush (party) after the service, a larger celebration took place the following day at the Clinton Plaza, a rather simple hall on the Lower East Side. The interior was nice enough. There was a large room, well lit, with plenty of space to move about, but it was by no means fancy. My parents were not able to afford an elaborate affair. Even at that age I perceived that whatever expense they had gone to had involved considerable sacrifice. My brother's Bar Mitzvah party, six years earlier, had been held in our apartment, but now that my father had been in business a little longer, my parents could afford more.

My father's real concern, though, was for the future, not a one-day celebration. This was best exemplified by the Bar Mitzvah present he gave me: an entire set of the Talmud translated into English. In 1959 such translations were not common. For me such a gift was priceless. Released in London by the Soncino Press, each volume was handsomely bound with leaves whose edges were gilded. This was my brand-new bicycle, my Encyclopaedia Britannica or whatever else my mind could have dreamed up. No doubt, I wanted the same toys that other thirteen-year-olds want, but this was in a category by itself, for this signified my entrance into the adult world. It symbolized the link with my past and the direction I was to take in the near future as a budding scholar of the Talmud.

The year of my Bar Mitzvah was my eighth and final year at the Light of Abraham Yeshiva.

One day I was called down to the principal's office. I walked in somewhat hesitantly. Dr. Heisler looked up from his black wooden desk, which was completely covered with papers, magazines and books. "Willy, how are you doing in your Gemara studies?" he asked. "Okay," I responded, wondering at the same time why he had asked. "You know I have a great deal of confidence in you. I've decided to give you a chance to show me that you deserve the confidence I have in you. Willy, I want you to learn the third chapter of the tractate *Baba Metziya* by heart. That's the one you're studying in class anyway." My legs went weak. By heart? How could I ever do that? Dr. Heisler's voice went on. "You know, you're thirteen years old now." I had celebrated my Bar Mitzvah a few weeks earlier and Dr. Heisler had been present, as he was at each of his students' Bar Mitzvahs. "You're a man and everything you do is written in G-d's Holy Book. I know you can do it. I'm sure you won't disappoint me."

That was all. Dr. Heisler told Miss Lazerwitz, the school secretary, to send in the next person. I walked out in a daze. "I can't do it," I thought. "Even Daddy would agree." The principal's last words reverberated in my head like the echo in a canyon and refused to melt into oblivion. "I know you won't disappoint me. . . . I know you won't disappoint me. . . . I know you won't disappoint me."

Within six months I had learned the chapter by heart, line for line, word for word. Initially, I experienced the same frustrations that had accompanied my earlier efforts when I began studying the Talmud. No matter how hard I tried, the material simply refused to stay in my head. I would read a paragraph in Aramaic, repeat the first two lines, and then my mind would go blank. Little by little, however, I made progress. Each evening my father would correct my mistakes. I often wondered what it was all for, this parrot-like memorizing.

Wealthy people often came to visit the school. In addition to being escorted around, these persons would sometimes express a desire to meet some of the students. When this happened, I would be called down to the principal's office. After I was introduced, Dr. Heisler would say: "Willy, what does the Gemara say on page forty-two, six lines from the bottom?" After I had correctly quoted and explained the passage, Dr. Heisler would beam. "You see, this is the type of student we produce here at the Light of Abraham Yeshiva."

That year was an exciting one. There was the yearbook to write, for example. Somehow, going to the local barbershop and to the Vigushin Fish Store, where my mother always shopped, to sell ads made me feel very important, a part of the adult world. Moreover, there was keen competition among the students to see who could raise the most money. Although we never gained financially from these sales, it became a status symbol that the pastry shop, the butcher store and the local grocery thought enough of you to contribute. It never occurred to me that they perceived the function of these advertisements somewhat differently.

And then there was writing compositions for the yearbook. My topic was Edgar Allan Poe. Of course the short biography underwent substantial revision by the teacher before it appeared in print, but that was of little consequence to us. It was important that something carrying our name be published.

The most exciting occasion, the one that capped the year, was graduation itself.

I had been a diligent student so that I could be admitted to a good high school, one that had both a good religious studies division and a fine secular studies department. Talmud, however, continued to be my best subject, and it appeared, at the time, that I was destined to make my mark in this area. Thus I was thrilled, but not surprised, when I was informed by both my teacher and by Dr. Heisler that I would receive the Rabbi Dr. Irving Glazer Memorial Prize for Excellence in Talmud. In practical terms, this meant that at graduation I would be singled out and given a savings bond and a certificate of achievement. My parents were not wealthy and so no plaque had ever been put up at the yeshiva in their honor, no testimonial dinners made on their behalf, and no honorary appointments had been offered them. Yes, my mother helped to make costumes for the school plays, and both my parents were active in the Parent-Teachers Association, but in their eyes their greatest wealth was their children.

The night of graduation was typical mid-June weather. A gentle breeze, whose warmth contained a strong hint of summer, greeted us as we left the house. My mother had prepared my finest suit, a beige gabardine with a checked gray vest and gold buttons that had tiny sailboats embossed on them.

We headed toward Columbus Avenue, for we were going by taxi. Taxis were a luxury for us, an experience to be anticipated and cherished. How I loved sitting in the vinyl-covered back seat, which, in the Checker cabs at least, was higher than those in the cars around us. Compared to the itchy straw that blanketed the hard seats on the IND subway line, it was sheer delight. Best of all was the speed at which the driver went, passing cars and buses by the dozen.

Within minutes we arrived at the auditorium, located in a public high school. Once inside, we checked our coats and I went quickly to my seat in a special section reserved for the graduates.

I opened the program outlining the order of things to come, quickly and eagerly scanning the pages for my name. I turned to the back of the four-page program, but it was not there either. I started again, carefully searching for the Talmud Prize listing. Jack Lowy and Joyce Berman were the recipients of the Hyman G. Kwalwasser Prize for Excellence in Religious and General Studies. That made sense. But wait! Something was wrong. Michael Wikler had won the prize for religious studies instead of Harry Finerman! Where was Harry's name? Suddenly I began to feel sick. I had found his name right next to the announcement of the winner of the Talmud Prize. My own name was nowhere. Tears of rage welled up in me. I looked around for Dr. Heisler, but he was sitting on the stage and therefore unapproachable. My family was smiling and looking with anticipation toward the stage.

The choir began singing the songs that we all knew. This was to be the last time I would hear the choir perform. In my agitated state, however, I hardly noticed. The valedictory addresses were followed by the presentation of the diplomas and awards. My name was called. As I stepped forward, I tripped and almost fell. The tears in my eyes had blurred my vision. I avoided Dr. Heisler's gaze as he handed me the diploma, and hurried back to my seat.

In a flashback, I saw myself standing in Dr. Heisler's office near the metal cabinet that was on the left when you walked in, reciting the portion about what the law was if a thief claimed to have stolen something but did not know from whom. The visitor, a rabbi from Mexico, was nodding approvingly, smiling at me in encouragement.

Suddenly I was jolted again into the present: "Harry Finerman, the Rabbi Dr. Irving Glazer Memorial Prize for Excellence in Talmud." The applause was deafening, louder than for any previous announcement, or so it seemed to me.

Shortly afterward the evening ended. I ran to my parents. My father was not there. He was talking with Dr. Heisler about the injustice done to me, said my mother, putting her arms around me. I saw my friends Michael and Harry walking together up the aisle laughing and talking. I looked away, hoping they wouldn't notice me standing forlornly next to my mother. Just then my father returned from the front of the auditorium. He was visibly angry. "Let's go, Willy. We're going home."

As we walked toward the subway (there was neither rush nor cause for celebration, so why take a cab?), I began to sob. "Why didn't I get the prize, Daddy? Why?" At first my father was silent. Then, apparently realizing that I needed some sort of answer, he said slowly, "There are some things which you will not be able to understand until you are older." Whereas on other occasions I might have accepted such a response, this time it was simply not enough. Deep down I knew what had happened. Finally I blurted out: "It's because we're not rich enough; because Mr. Wikler and Mr. Finerman have more money than us, right?"

We were standing at the corner now, waiting for the light to change. My father adjusted his tie and cleared his throat before speaking. "Willy, I'm going to tell you something now that I hope you will remember for the rest of your life: You won that prize. You won it." "But I didn't get it," I broke in, "Harry got it!" "What did he get?" replied my father. "A twenty-five-dollar bond? That's nothing. Unimportant. Look at the knowledge you have. He got the prize, but you know the Gemara. Nobody can ever take that away from you and that's what counts."

The way my father handled

that situation was typical of the way he approached everything in life—love and reason intertwined and inseparable. We had little money, and as a result I received few of the material benefits that come with growing up in more comfortable surroundings. I can count on my fingers the toys I had as a child—an erector set, a John Gnagy paint set, a group of plastic race horses that moved forward one space every time a spinner landed on them, and perhaps a few more items. And yet my father more than made up for these "deprivations," for he gave of himself. He gave Mark and me his time, energy, love and devotion.

Virtually every Sunday was reserved for "the children": the Bronx Zoo, the Bronx Botanical Gardens, Van Cortlandt Park—even when we visited relatives there was always something in it for Mark and me. There were Uncle Herman and Aunt Deborah, for instance, who lived in the Bronx. At the end of the long, dusty ride on the D train we would eat rum cake and cookies and watch TV.

I vividly recall being there one Sunday afternoon, while they all talked about the Nazis. Nazis? What did I know about them? Nothing really, except that they had killed Jews, many of them. This plus my experiences on the block represented my understanding of contemporary hatred for us. In addition, many of our holidays dealt with enemies of the Jews, who only through G-d's intervention had been thwarted in their evil intentions. Haman, the adviser to the Persian king, Ahasuerus, had plotted against the Jews as had Antiochus, the Greek king; the Egyptians had enslaved us, the Romans had destroyed our Temple, and so on. This led to the feeling that such animosity was inevitable and universal and that individual Jews were powerless to affect the situation. Only G-d could help us.

In such an atmosphere religion naturally assumed tremendous importance. It was all we had and yet it was so much.

Sometimes we would go for a ride in Uncle Herman's old black car, built in the late 1940s, with two little windows in the back and three windows on each side. The interior had a certain smell that old cars usually get—nothing unpleasant, simply a combination of cloth seats and somewhat cracked leather armrests, mixed with people and the odor of an engine burning. I would sit in the back looking out the small windows as the branches of the trees passed by overhead. Generally we went to a park. Once we went to a high school football game to see my cousin Ernie play. I was about seven years old, and although the game made little sense to me, I felt comfortable in the knowledge that we were all there together as one family.

Each free Sunday, from the time I was eleven years old, my parents and I took a subway to the last stop on the line. Once there, we would get out and walk around the neighborhood. There are hundreds of miles of track in the New York City subway system and dozens of different subway lines, and it was a long time before we exhausted our options.

The minute I got on the train, I ran to the front to peer through the wire-enforced window into the near-total darkness of the tunnel ahead. As I stood there, I held on to the gold-colored door handle on my right halfway down the door, and moved it from side to side (it was always a little loose), pretending I was the engineer. Sometimes the train would have to slow down because of a red light or a train ahead, and I would get a special sense of satisfaction out of knowing the reason for the delay while the other passengers wondered. At times there were as many as six or seven children jockeying for a better view, thus making it impossible for the late-comers to see anything. If that happened, I would simply have to content myself with looking through the subway window whenever the train burst out of the tunnel into the brightness of day.

The trains were old and swayed crazily from side to side to a rhythm of their own. Naked yellow light bulbs competed for space with large black propeller fans, whose capacity for moving the soot and hot air around was a mixed blessing even on the warmest of days. And the sound! Instead of one loud muffled roar, there were a hundred and one noises at once, ranging from the squeaky sound of trains changing tracks to the creaking sounds emanating from the metal straps badly in need of oil for their hinges. There were no announcements, no one to tell you what stop was coming up. No warnings were given to watch the closing doors, though one learned soon enough. The maps located in the cars were few and far between, and the conductors seemed less approachable, almost as though they lived in another world. Each subway line had its own peculiarities. The BMT had three-seater benches, and the IND had two single seats in each car set aside from the rest.

Some areas we visited were similar to ours while others were not. There were wealthy neighborhoods and there were poor ones. Old and new parts of the city, Jewish sections and Italian ones, tree-lined streets and garbage-filled neighborhoods. "This is Canarsie," my father would say, as we looked out over a vast expanse of marshland dotted with a few lonely houses here and there. So this was the place my fifth-grade teacher had threatened to send me if I did not behave. "This is Wall Street, Willy." He would point to a building and begin to explain what the Stock Exchange was, but I scarcely listened, for he had promised to take me on the nearby Staten Island ferry and my mind was racing ahead, already imagining what it would be like to feel the water under my feet, separated from me only by a planked wooden deck.

Wherever I went, whatever I did, in those early years, it was always with my parents. Sometimes Mark would come along, too, but being six years older than I, he was a teenager and often was busy with other things. Although my mother was usually with us, it is my father whose presence stands out. My mother was a very quiet woman. She did not speak out often, preferring to leave the decision-making to my father. Her childhood had been a sheltered one. She had grown up in Antwerp, Belgium, in comfortable surroundings. The war had shattered that life, as it had disrupted the lives of so many millions of Jews who, although they did not perish, must be listed among the casualties of that period. In her case, it was a matter of becoming somewhat shy. When we were small, she took care of us all the time, giving totally and selflessly. As my brother and I grew older and became more assertive, she receded into the background and my father assumed the functions of both disciplinarian and role model.

At the age of sixteen, my brother Mark went to Israel for a year. Born in Belgium in 1939, he had been forced to flee, at the age of eighteen months, with my parents, when the Nazis began deporting Jews in large numbers from Antwerp.

My parents and other members of my mother's family had packed in the middle of the night (each person was allowed to take one suitcase) and left the city on a wagon, bound for Paris. The road was filled with refugees, and it was necessary to pull over to the side many times as German planes strafed the area.

For the next year they lived in different French cities—Paris, Bordeaux and Marseille—always one step ahead of the Germans. On one occasion my father learned of an apartment that had suddenly become available in what was considered a safe area in Marseille. An entire apartment was virtually unheard of. My father rushed over to the address. By the time he arrived, the landlady had already rented it to another Jewish family. His heart heavy, my father returned to the cramped room to break the news to my mother. He later learned that the next day two SS officers had come to that very apartment and taken its occupants to central headquarters, from where they were sent east to Auschwitz.

Finally, my family left Marseille and moved into the forests of southern France, from where they eventually succeeded in escaping into neutral Switzerland.

I was born in Zurich in 1945. Because we had relatives in the United States, we were able to secure visas, arriving here in 1946.

Mark, my brother, had spent the first six years of his life hiding and running from one place to another. The vicissitudes of the war must surely have played a role in the restlessness that became a part of his personality in early adolescence. He became friendly with a group of neighborhood youths who were members of an intensely Zionist organization. Almost every night was spent at meetings of the group. And then one day my brother announced his intention to leave for the Holy Land. My father's face turned white. "You can't go. Why, you're only sixteen years old." But my brother was adamant. "Israel is a place where I could do something meaningful, maybe work on a kibbutz." Living on a kibbutz invariably meant hard work, difficult conditions and danger from the Arab "fedayeen," as the raiders were called, who preyed on these front-line settlements.

The day of Mark's departure was a bright sunny September morning in 1955. Everyone in the house rose early. That special tension that always seems to accompany trips was there and seemed to blend in perfectly with the brisk autumn air that entered through the partially opened window in the bedroom that we shared. I looked over at his bed. It was already empty. He had gone into the bathroom to wash up. "Yes," I thought, "it'll be empty now for good." As a ten-year-old, I still saw things in black and white. Either my brother was going away for good or he was returning at a specific time, and since he had not given a time, then that must mean that his absence would be permanent.

I washed, dressed quickly and said my prayers carefully, being certain to keep in mind my brother as well as myself as I uttered the words. Breakfast was eaten in almost complete silence. My parents' eyes were bleary. They both had their coffee first. My father looked unusually grim and my mother appeared uncertain and nervous. My brother said not a word.

After eating, we said grace and got ready to go. My father dragged the heavy brown suitcase with the tear in the bottom out the door and half-pushed, half-carried it down the narrow hall to the elevator. The broken leather straps with their metal buckles made a scratchy noise as they banged against the tiled floor. My brother walked behind my father carrying another brown suitcase, this one made of cloth and held together by rope. My mother and I brought up the rear carrying a small travel bag and other odds and ends. Somehow we managed to squeeze everything, including ourselves, into the elevator.

Once outside, my father hailed a yellow Checker cab and instructed the driver to take us to the dockyards in Brooklyn. Brooklyn was like another world to me, a place one went to only on special occasions, such as visits to relatives, weddings and school trips. The fact that the boat was leaving from there seemed therefore appropriate to me. We headed down Columbus Avenue to Fifty-ninth Street, turning east there. As I glanced out the window at Central Park South, I remembered a trip I had once made to a dentist there, a specialist. What other connection could I have to anyone who could afford to live in the Essex House or any of the other luxury buildings, whose elegant canopies stretched toward the street?

In a few minutes we were on the East River Drive heading toward the Brooklyn Bridge. No one spoke. Everyone was either looking straight ahead or staring out a window. It was as though we were playing out a drama that no one wanted to see end. I could already imagine my brother stalking off, my father standing ramrod straight, with my mother fighting back tears. I wanted to tell the driver, "Turn around, it's all a mistake," but of course that was foolish. It was no error. It had already been decided. Besides, we were already beginning the downward slope on the bridge into Brooklyn.

We entered an area of deserted streets with warehouses of turn-of-the-century vintage, whose tall shadows blocked the morning light. Finally, we arrived at the docks. The driver pulled the suitcases from the trunk, depositing them at the base of the slatted wooden walk that led to the ship. My father paid the driver and we walked toward the boat.

It was a large ship, with the letters "ZIM" emblazoned in

blue on its side. The largest vessel I had ever been on before that day was the Circle Line boat that took tourists around Manhattan Island, and so I was full of excitement at the prospect of exploring this one. We climbed a few stairs to the dock and stood there, not quite sure of what to do next.

Presently, a man wearing a tight polo shirt with horizontal black and white stripes emerged. "Yes, what can I do you for?" he inquired. My brother gave his name to the man, who, I noticed, was holding a list in his right hand. He checked off Mark's name and, pointing to his left, said, "Cabin 41. Straight through the door, to your left. The key's in the room."

We walked through the door and down a narrow hall until we came to No. 41. It was a cramped room, whose sole furniture consisted of two wooden chairs, painted off-white, a small sink under a dusty mirror and a double-decker bed. My brother put his suitcases down. We all left the room and went back outside into the fresh air. There were at least two hours left before departure. My father began talking quite suddenly to Mark: "If you get seasick, try to remember that it's all in your mind and if you feel very bad lie down in your bed." My mother joined in, too. "Did you pack in your toothbrush? How about your sweater?"

The boat began to fill up as more people arrived. Before I knew it, the time had come for us to depart. As we turned to go, my father proffered his hand, and then, as my brother shook it, pulled him forward and embraced him tightly. "You'll write us, won't you?" he said tensely. And then: "You know, even though I don't agree with what you're doing, I am your father and I love you." My brother, who always acted the role of tough guy, dropped his mask. His voice soft, filled with emotion, he said, "Don't worry, Daddy, I'll stay in touch. I'll write you every week." Turning

100

next to me and my mother, he kissed us both goodbye. I wanted to say something to him, but the man in the polo shirt was coming toward us again. "Are you going or staying?" he yelled. We headed down the ramp and joined the crowd of people below, all of whom were waving to those on deck.

We looked for my brother, but were unable to find him at first. "There he is!" I shouted, pulling my father's arm excitedly and pointing to the left. He was standing near the stern of the boat by a small iron gate. I had recognized his navy-blue French beret, which, as usual, was set at a rakish angle on his head. All three of us began waving at him and he at us, but I was not sure whether he really saw us or was simply waving at the crowd. The smile on his face seemed frozen, as though a photographer had told him to say "Cheese." A tiny figure among many, he looked so alone that a wave of pity overcame me. I wanted so much to be with him, despite my father's obvious disapproval.

As the boat pulled away and headed out toward the Atlantic Ocean, my strong sense of emptiness was heightened by the jostling of the crowd of strangers as we all began to leave.

My brother was gone for a whole year. He kept his word and wrote every week, but that only made me notice his absence even more. His presence had always been a part of my life. He had occupied the fourth and now empty chair at mealtimes. He had slept in my room, and we had gone to synagogue together. We had fought as brothers do, but we had also shared many pleasant experiences. We had gone to the movies together, played ball with each other and so on, but above all we were branches of the same tree.

In relation to some of the other holidays, Chanukah was a minor holiday. It commemorated an event that had occurred in post-Biblical times. Yet in certain fundamental ways its significance was considerable. First, it was a family holiday. For eight evenings everyone sang songs together, performed ceremonies together and spent a few hours together. Moreover, it was the type of holiday that children loved and identified with. There were special games to be played, special foods to be eaten, presents for all, etc. Finally, Chanukah happens to coincide with Christmas. The stores announced, "Only seven days left until Christmas." Gift-wrapping without little Santa Clauses or Christmas bells became scarce. How could one send a Chanukah gift with pictures of Rudolph, the red-nosed reindeer, on it? But, as a child, what most concerned me was that there was something out there which I could not identify with. The occasion it celebrated was one that I associated with prejudice toward my people. The person whose birth had become a holiday for hundreds of millions of people throughout the world was one whom I was accused of having killed.

Yet Christmas itself seemed so innocuous when I walked by the large windows on the ground floor of my building and looked in upon neighbors celebrating the holiday. How nice and warm it seemed with everyone sitting around the tree talking, playing and laughing. The gaily colored shiny metal balls caught the light of the flashing electric candles as they swung gently back and forth. Something was going on there of which I, always so attached to ceremony, could not partake; not if I lived to be a thousand years could I ever feel comfortable in such a setting.

Enter Chanukah: Compared to the pomp and circumstance that surrounded Christmas, it seemed almost like a consolation prize at first. By the time I was through learning about it, however, I felt otherwise, for Chanukah was a tale of heroic struggle by a small band of Maccabees against the mighty Syrian-Greeks led by King Antiochus. Antiochus was a particularly repressive ruler who installed his own deities in the Holy Temple and elsewhere and decreed that Jews and all other foreign subjects must bow down to them. But a group of Jews led by Mattathias, who was a High Priest, and his five sons resisted. They fled to the mountains, hid in caves and battled the Syrian-Greeks for three years, finally emerging victorious with the capture of the Temple of Jerusalem in 165 B.C.E.

As we learned the story in school, there was only sufficient pure oil bearing the seal of the holy priest for a lamp to burn one night in the Temple when the Maccabees entered it, but a miracle occurred and the oil lasted eight days. To commemorate what was surely a sign from G-d to His people, we celebrated the festival for eight nights. The first night, one candle was lit; the following night, two; and so on until the last night, when the light of eight candles brightened our living room. Actually, it was twenty-four, for each of us—my father, my brother and I—had his own menorah, or candelabra, over which we said the blessings and lit the candles.

Usually, I came home about 4:30 or 5:00 P.M., tired and hungry. But on the twenty-fifth day of Kislev (one of the

Hebrew months) I rushed home, my heart and soul full of anticipation, for it was the first night of the holiday. The menorahs were already on the window sill, resting on a piece of cardboard so that the dripping wax would not stick to the sill.

As night fell, we all said the daily evening prayers. Then, as we stood in front of the window, my father struck a wooden match and lit one of the candles. This candle was to be the shammes, the servant, to light all the other candles. As always, our recognition of the commandment we were about to fulfill was preceded by a benediction: "Blessed art Thou, O Lord our G-d, King of the Universe, who has sanctified us by Thy commandments and commanded us to kindle the light of Chanukah." Then, in a voice filled with fervor and emotion, my father continued, ". . . O Lord our G-d who worked miracles for our fathers in days of old, at this season." And finally, the blessing traditionally said at the start of any new holiday: "Blessed art Thou . . . who has kept us in life, and has preserved us, and enabled us to reach this season." That last fact in itself was a miracle, for I had been taught and believed that every day and every moment I lived was a direct result of G-d's mercy.

At this point, my father began lighting the candles, all the while singing:

We kindle these lights because of the miracles, the deliverances, and the wonders which Thou didst work for our fathers in those days and in this season, through Thy holy priests.

During all these eight days of Chanukah these lights are sacred. We are not permitted to make any profane use of them; but we are only allowed to look at them; in order that we may give thanks unto Thy great name for Thy miracles, Thy deliverances, and Thy wonders.

104

As I looked at my parents, the flames cast an eerie yet warm glow upon their faces and I was gripped by an overpowering feeling of deep love and affection. It was they who had created in me love for G-d and awareness of His spirituality.

Each one of us said the blessings separately and lit the candles. Then we stepped back and began singing a special song commemorating the holiday.

Perhaps it was the flickering candles themselves, or perhaps simply the fact that the holiday came but once a year. For whatever reason, a certain warmth, a certain closeness, was present as we stood there, singing and swaying gently to and fro, each of us knowing that all the words we were singing were familiar to us, each of us sensing that the other was thinking similar thoughts. Although we sang in Hebrew, we knew the meaning of every word:

"O Fortress, Rock of my salvation, unto Thee it is becoming to give praise: let my house of prayer be restored and I will there offer Thee thanksgivings." ("And if I were there, would You allow me to enter?" I thought. "Would I be worthy of reflecting upon and honoring Your majesty? How can I convince You of my sincerity, of my desire to come close to and be at one with You? To rejoice at Your earthly altar?") And then, singing louder and more fervently, we continued:

> To His holy shrine He brought me,
> yet even there I found no peace,
> for the oppressor came and led me captive,
> because I had worshiped strange gods,
> I drank from the wine of confusion,
> I had nearly perished when Babylon's end drew close;
> through Zerubbabel I was saved after seventy years.

Of all the stories in the

Bible perhaps none was so fascinating as the saga of the Jews during and immediately after their stay in Egypt. For 210 years they had been enslaved. The Ten Plagues G-d had visited upon the Egyptians temporarily persuaded Pharaoh to let the Israelites go free. The oppression, the miracles and the happy ending were a familiar story to me, but Passover was different from the other holidays.

The extensive preparations began early. About a week before the holiday, Mark and I would accompany my father to the Lower East Side to purchase matzohs, the unleavened bread that was eaten on Passover. The passage in Exodus 12:20 read: "Ye shall eat nothing leavened; in all your settlements shall ye eat unleavened bread." When the Israelites had finally been freed by Pharaoh, they wanted to leave as quickly as possible, partly at Pharaoh's urging and partly out of fear that he would change his mind once again. As a result, they did not have even enough time to allow the bread that they had baked as provisions for the journey to leaven. As a remembrance of this, the Torah commanded that throughout the entire seven-day holiday the Jews eat only the thin, wafer-like matzoh that the Israelites had eaten.

We headed to a place where matzohs were hand-baked. We walked down a narrow side street crowded with shoppers. The briny smell of pickles filled the air. Here, as in other, older parts of the city, the squares of concrete that made up the sidewalk were uneven, some higher than the rest, many of them cracked or broken. The tenements, five or six stories in height, looked dingy and gloomy, their depressing appearance improved only slightly by the multicolored clothing that hung over many of the fire escapes. This was the place where so many Jews had begun their lives in America. It seemed fitting therefore that whenever we went to the Lower East Side it was for something connected with our religion—to visit a religious bookstore, to eat in Turk's Kosher Dairy Restaurant, to buy religious books or to purchase items for the different holidays.

We stopped in front of one of these tenements and went down a crooked flight of stone steps until we came to a large gray metal door. Opening it, we found ourselves looking at about twenty men and women standing next to a long table assembly-style. Some were flattening out the dough; others were using a small machine that gave it its round shape. No one was talking; everyone was working. Every few minutes a thin, energetic-looking man would come running over to the assembly line with a long wooden pole and drape the shaped dough on it. The room was crowded with other people engaged in a variety of undefined activities, and in order to get through the man would yell, "Matzohs! Matzohs!" His function was to bring the matzohs to the oven.

From where I was standing I could see the flames from the oven. A giant of a man with a beard to match was standing by it putting in the matzohs. He was wearing a sleeveless undershirt beneath a pair of large tzizis. His lips were pursed and his face taut with determination as he concentrated on his task. The flames cast an eerie glow over his body, glistening with sweat. The scene gave me a clear comprehension of what the Bible meant when it said in Exodus 12:39: "And they baked unleavened cakes of the dough which they had brought forth out of Egypt, for it was not leavened; because they were thrust out of Egypt and could not tarry, neither had they prepared for themselves any victual."

My father watched the oven carefully as a batch was put in for him, for it was considered proper to supervise the preparation of one's own unleavened bread. As a child in Poland, my father had helped his father bake the matzoh in the small town in which he lived.

Afterward we went into the next room, where the matzohs were put into a large white cake box and tied with string. If a matzoh was broken, it could no longer be used for making a blessing at the beginning of the meal (although it could still be eaten during the meal itself). All around the room were wooden shelves on top of which lay similar boxes reserved for those who might not be able to be present at the moment of baking.

Perhaps no one in our family was busier than my mother in the weeks before Passover. The entire house had to be cleaned from top to bottom. No chometz (leaven) was permitted to be in the house, and here the Torah had been specific: "Seven days shall there be no leaven found in your houses; for whosoever eateth that which is leavened that soul shall be cut off from the congregation of Israel" (Exodus 12:19). Chometz was all food containing leaven. Thus any one of the following grains—wheat, barley, spelt, oats or rye —that had been in water for a minimum of eighteen minutes was considered leavened and therefore forbidden.

My mother would begin her shopping weeks ahead of time to avoid the last-minute rush. All products bought had to have a Kosher for Passover label, whether it be canned carrots, coffee, candies, sodas or toothpaste. Moreover, the label had to be certified by a reliable rabbi. Many of the products, such as sugar and salt, contained no chometz, but it was considered good to have the certifying label simply because it meant that the products' preparation had been supervised by a rabbi and that no one with chometz had been seen near them.

In addition to the shopping and cleaning, all the dishes and silverware used during the year were put away in a closet that was taped shut for the entire holiday. Special dishes, silverware, pots and pans that had been kept aside for the holiday were taken out and dusted off. The effect was total. It was as though we were moving into another apartment for a week. I even had to give away my parakeet for the holiday since the food he ate was chometz. There were also many foods that were generally eaten only on Passover, such as macaroons and chocolate-covered matzohs, and this made the holiday something to be eagerly anticipated, though by the end of the week I could hardly wait until I could again bite into a fresh roll.

The night before Passover eve, immediately after dark, we symbolically "searched" for leaven. My father would say the blessing: ". . . who has sanctified us with His commandments and commanded us concerning the destruction of the leaven." Then, with my brother holding the candle, we would go from room to room. Earlier in the day my mother had put pieces of bread in various places for my father to "find." The small linen doily which covered one of the end tables in the living room usually sheltered one small piece of bread; the plastic tablecloth that lay on the weekday dinner table in my room shielded yet another. Holding open a brown paper bag, my father would sweep the bread into it, making sure not to miss a single crumb.

The candle, our sole source of light, drew us closer together as we clustered around it looking here and there. No one spoke until after the investigation. Because it was possible that there still was some chometz in the house that had been overlooked, perhaps crumbs from a cookie I had eaten that had dropped to the ground unnoticed, my father would make the following declaration: "All leaven and chometz in my possession which I did not see and which I failed to destroy, let it be worthless as is the dust of the earth."

The bread that had been "found" was put aside until the following morning, when it was burnt, for after a third of the day had passed it was forbidden to have any bread in the house.

Finally, all preparations having been completed, the holiday began that evening at our synagogue. Inside, we created an island in the midst of the alien world, an island of holiness and peace, of beauty and joy. As we sang the ancient and soul-stirring melodies, the outside world existed but at a distance. We were not really a part of it. And as we left the synagogue for the short walk home, our sacred island enveloped us, for everyone was already thinking of what lay ahead—the Seder, the Passover evening meal. In terms of the unity of the family and in terms of our family's pre-eminent role in my life, no holiday was as important. Furthermore, no holiday had a ceremony that was so rich and varied in every detail as the Seder meal. The word "Seder" meant "order," so named because the meal followed a specific ritual unique to this holiday.

As I walked into our apartment, I could already detect the sharp odor of horseradish that we would later eat to commemorate the bitter times and suffering endured by the Israelites during their enforced stay in Egypt. My mother was running in and out of the kitchen making last-minute preparations. Everything had to be perfect that night. The table in the living room was covered with a multitude of ceremonial dishes. Next to each setting was a Haggadah (the word means "telling"), the book which described the story of our forefathers' deliverance. Here and there, between the individual settings and in other empty spaces, I could see parts of the plastic Passover tablecloth with its narrative drawings. Near the head of the table were depicted the pyramids surrounded by Israelites dragging huge slabs of stone, urged on by whip-wielding Egyptian taskmasters. Farther down were drawings of the various foods that we would eat as the meal progressed, and across from them was a picture of Moses leading us through the Red Sea to safety from the pursuing legions of Pharaoh's army.

The thrilling story of the Exodus from Egypt would be told that evening by my father. The living room easy chair had been pushed over to the head of the table, where he always sat. Three pillows lay on the chair, a large one for the seat and two smaller ones for each side. In this way my father was able to recline comfortably. This was considered a symbol of liberty, for who but a truly free man could afford to dine in such luxury?

Everyone's goblet was filled with wine as my father began reciting the blessing. Significantly, the wine we used was red. We had learned in school that in the past, when Jews had been slanderously accused of using human blood on the night of the Passover, it had been considered wise in some communities to use only white wine. Altogether we drank four cups at different points during the Seder, each of which symbolized the four freedoms mentioned in Exodus 6:6–7, where G-d had said: "I will bring you out [from Egypt] . . . deliver you . . . redeem you . . . and I will take you to Me for a people."

Next my mother would bring a large basin and some water to my father for the traditional washing of the hands.

111

Then my father would take a cold boiled potato, dip it into some salt water and give each of us a piece to eat. This potato, growing as it had in the ground, symbolized the spring season, times of plenty and our faith in the future. After that my father took the middle matzoh (there were three, one on top of the other), which lay in front of him covered by a napkin, and broke it in half, leaving one half in its place and placing the other half in the napkin underneath one of the pillows behind him.

Some say the three matzohs represent the three Patriarchs Abraham, Isaac and Jacob, and others that they are symbols of the Kohanim, Levites and Israelites, the three different tribal groups that make up the Jewish people. These interpretations, fascinating as they were when I learned them in class, were of little importance at that particular moment. My eyes were riveted upon that pillow on the chair behind which my father had placed the half-piece of matzoh, the afikomen.

The afikomen, which took the place of the Paschal lamb that had been eaten in the days of the Temple, was to be eaten as the last course of the meal, but not before my brother and I had a chance to hide it and withhold it from our father in return for a promise of a gift for each of us. This game had developed over the centuries as a way of keeping the children interested in the Seder.

My father would leave the living room for a minute on some pretext, and that would be our signal. One of us would leap from his chair, grab the matzoh wrapped in the cloth napkin and stow it away. One year it was behind an old print of three horses standing in a forest, which hung on the living room wall. Another time we shoved it between the folds of the living room curtains. My father, when the time for eating the afikomen came, would very convincingly feign anger and distress upon discovering that the afikomen was no longer in its place. "Where did you put it, boys? You know that's not right." But the twinkling eyes and broad hint of a smile bespoke his awareness. "You'll have to look for it, Daddy," we would say, and off he went, with my mother assisting, going through every room and eventually giving up.

He rarely succeeded in finding it, and though he would never spoil our fun by admitting it, I don't believe he wanted to, for the rules were that only if he failed to come up with the afikomen were we entitled to a prize of our choice. Only once can I remember this scenario being changed. We had hidden the afikomen beneath a corner of the faded, blue carpet in the living room. We watched with gleeful apprehension as Daddy walked by the spot several times. Then, just as he was about to give up, he stepped right smack on the afikomen. There was a sharp crack as the matzoh broke. My brother and I groaned with disappointment. My father was rather annoyed, for even though the matzoh could still be eaten, he did not think it was a very good hiding place. As a result our present that year was not quite what we had hoped for.

All this, however, occurred later. At this point we were still at the beginning of the meal. Together we all picked up the large china dish containing a bone and an egg and proclaimed: "I now begin to fulfill the divine commandment of relating the story of the Exodus from Egypt, as prescribed by Jewish law."

The bone, which was roasted, was yet another symbol of the Paschal lamb of Temple days, and the egg was the traditional Jewish symbol of mourning, to remind us that our Temple was no more.

We began singing in Aramaic:

This is the bread of suffering that our forefathers ate in the land of Egypt.

Let all those who are hungry enter and eat from it and all those who are in distress come and celebrate Passover.

Now we celebrate it here, but next year we hope to have our celebration in Israel.

This year we are servants here, but next year we hope to be free in Israel.

It never occurred to me to ask why we didn't simply pick up and go to Israel. Maybe the religious context in which this wish was expressed caused me to believe that G-d alone could determine our future. Even so, my heart would swell a bit as I thought about the idea of living in the Promised Land. The melody itself propelled my thoughts, sad at first, reminding me of the glory of ancient Israel, then going up a few octaves, picking up tempo as the hope for the future was articulated.

Our cups were filled again, and now it was my turn to be the center of attention. I rose from my chair and began reciting the Four Questions: "Why is this night different from all other nights?" I then proceeded to point out the four distinctions: that on this night we were not permitted to eat leavened bread, that we could eat only bitter herbs, that we dipped certain foods twice into other substances, and that we reclined in our chairs instead of merely sitting.

When I was young, my brother had asked these questions. Now he listened while I tried my best not to miss a single word. After I finished and sat down my father began telling the story of Passover, how we were slaves until the Holy One freed us, and that had it not been for Him we would still be in Egypt today. The spirits of Abraham, Isaac and

Jacob moved among us as my father read. I felt totally at peace. In a soothing singsong melody my father described how in every generation from the beginning of time there had been those who had oppressed us. And yet, through the mercy of the Creator, we had been spared and delivered from the clutches of our enemies. The white gown with the frilled collar worn by my father, the candles, the beautifully arranged table with the holiday foods made the stories of affliction seem distant, far, far away. But of course I knew them to be true, and I looked upon the peaceful contrast of our Seder meal as the happy ending to those tales.

We had survived, had we not? Moreover, we had kept our traditions intact, for we were performing the laws tonight just as our people had done in Palestine, Babylonia, Germany, Russia, Poland, Spain and wherever else Jews had lived. The dark nights of the Crusades, the oppression of the Czars and the flames of the crematoria had all failed to quench our determination to survive as Jews.

I was a link in an unbroken chain of tradition. Who could bear to break it? It was inconceivable. The anguished cries of those who had perished in the name of G-d through the centuries could not so easily be forgotten. For what purpose had they died? And what would they think? They were watching and remembering.

And as my father quietly talked about the giving of the Torah on Mount Sinai, I recalled having learned in school that every Jew had been present on that occasion, the souls of all the Jews who had ever lived and those who were still to be born. How could one deny or even question such a magnificent heritage?

I was simply a soldier in an army, one believer among many, and why should G-d favor me with any special sort of attention? Besides, was not the highest form of service

115

that which anticipated no reward? At the same time, it was an important army in whose ranks I marched. The responsibilities of fulfilling the commandments were no small affair. And everyone knew that G-d was all-seeing and all-knowing, that not even the smallest detail escaped His attention. Everything was set down in the Book of Judgment, the book that would be opened to my page when the day of reckoning came.

Our religion was life itself, it was that which gave meaning to my existence. If it was more an affair of the soul than of the body, then that simply made the soul more alive, more tangible, so much so that it gave meaning to the very actions of my body—my lips parting in prayer, my hands moving upward in supplication to the Almighty, my legs squeezed together as I stood in synagogue, my eyes closing hard as I concentrated upon what I was saying, my head bowing at different points in the service. Thus the G-dlike holiness of the soul was the flame that gave the body its warmth, the force that gave it direction and purpose, thereby helping me strive toward achieving the ideal of fusing body and soul into one powerful form, a form which made possible direct communication with the Holy One.

The Seder itself was an example of how the concrete and the abstract blended together. My father would pick up the little plate containing the horseradish and say: "This bitter herb which we eat, what is it for? It is because the Egyptians embittered the lives of our forefathers in Egypt." The symbolism was not lost on me, for later on we would eat some matzoh with horseradish on it and the bitter taste would linger on afterward.

In my Haggadah were unforgettable drawings of the Ten Plagues suffered by the Egyptians: the water turning to blood, the locusts swarming over the land, the darkness setting in over the fields and houses of the Egyptians, and the look of horror on the Egyptian mother's face as she pointed an accusing finger upward at G-d for having slain her first-born son. Who dared ignore the dark threat of punishment for transgressions implied by these images?

Everyone at the table would recite the Hebrew names of the plagues in unison. As each plague was mentioned, we dipped our forefinger once lightly into the cup of wine that was before us. This was to indicate that in the midst of our joy at gaining freedom we still sorrowed at the spilling of blood, even that of our enemies. Throughout the storytelling my father encouraged Mark and me to ask questions about the holiday and the different ceremonies that were being performed. In the days before Passover, he had stayed up late each night carefully reviewing the laws and customs, trying to anticipate the lines of inquiry that we would pursue at the table.

We usually completed the first part of the Seder by 9:30 P.M., or after two hours. Then we ate dinner. After such a long wait, the food tasted even better than was ordinarily the case. The meal itself was simple and traditional— chicken soup with a potato or two in it, a piece of chicken with perhaps a vegetable. Afterward we said grace, making certain to add the special prayer that was said on Passover.

The Seder concluded with the ceremony in honor of Elijah the Prophet. The nicest cup we owned, made of silver and richly decorated with a Star of David and bunches of grapes representing the wine drunk that night, stood in the center of the table, filled to the brim with wine. My brother or I would go to the door that led out to the hall, open it wide and prop a chair against it so that it could not close. This was our invitation to Elijah the Prophet, who, according to legend, would herald the coming of the Messiah, to enter our

117

apartment and drink from the cup that we had set aside for him.

I asked my father, "Daddy, how come we can't see Elijah and how can he come into everyone's home at the same time?" "This is a miracle that only G-d can make," my father replied. Then, perhaps seeing a glimmer of doubt in my face, he went on, "If G-d can create the entire world, bring ten plagues on the Egyptians, and split the Red Sea so that we can escape, then this miracle is an easy one by comparison."

I still had one last question: "How come the cup is still full if he drinks from it?" "Because," my father responded, "he drinks so little that you can't notice it."

For a child of eight or nine such explanations made religion even more beautiful and intriguing than it already was. It made the traditions that I possessed seem more unique, in addition to giving me a spiritual world to which I could retreat when life became too complicated or unpleasant.

This ceremony was actually an act of faith in more ways than one, for our neighborhood was not a very safe one, as the door chain that was always latched at night attested to. Yet this night was traditionally known as a night of safety, one in which G-d watched over us even more than at other times, and it was indicative of our faith in Him that we performed this ritual without fear.

The last portion of the Seder was perhaps the most fun for Mark and me. This was the time for singing songs about the holiday and our freedom. By this time we had already drunk the fourth cup of wine and everyone was beginning to feel a bit drowsy. We needed something to perk us up, and the fast, snappy tunes were most welcome. The last two hymns had been composed especially to hold the interest of children at the Seder. The first one was in the form of a riddle song, which began as follows:

Who knows what is one?
I know one—One is our G-d in heaven and on earth.

Who knows two?
I know two—the two tablets of law.

Who knows three?
I know three—three Patriarchs (Abraham, Isaac, Jacob).

Who knows four?
I know four—four mothers (Sarah, Rebecca, Rachel and Leah).

And so it went. Each number referred to something different: seven to the days of the week culminating in the Sabbath, eight symbolizing the circumcision of every Jewish male on the eighth day, twelve representing the twelve tribes of Israel, and finally thirteen, the number of different attributes possessed by the Lord. Each time a new number was mentioned, all the preceding numbers and their phrases would be repeated as well. My brother and I delighted in singing the song as quickly as possible while making certain not to miss a single word, as my parents smiled indulgently.

The evening concluded with the singing, in Aramaic, of "One Kid," the story of a father who bought a baby goat, only to have it consumed by a cat, which was in turn bitten by a dog, who was hit by a stick for his foul deed. Following that, the fire burned the stick and was itself drowned in water, which was drunk by an ox, who was killed by a slaughterer. The angel of death killed the slaughterer, only to meet his own end at the hands of the Almighty.

Some scholars have interpreted this song as an allegory of how G-d makes the punishment fit the crime, but for Mark and me it was simply one last opportunity to celebrate the holiday. The clipped Aramaic words lent themselves to a rapid, staccato-like rendition. Faster and faster went the words, and then suddenly the evening ended and everyone reluctantly went to bed.

As a child I had the usual fears—complete darkness in the room, strange sounds coming from outside the house. On this night, however, I felt totally at peace and unafraid. The spirit of G-d protected us as on no other night of the year. It was the Night of Watching.

My summers were spent in an Orthodox boys' camp high up in New York State's Catskill Mountains. In all, I went there for nine summers from the time I was six until shortly after my fifteenth birthday.

In many respects Camp Tikvath Shalom was like any other summer camp. We played baseball and basketball, worked on arts and crafts, and had our ears and nails inspected by the camp mother before being allowed into the dining room. Before we sat at the dining room table we washed our hands ritually. After that we could be seated and eat.

Saying grace after meals was identical to the procedure followed at the Light of Abraham Yeshiva with one important exception—it was competitive. As an incentive, a prize, usually a watermelon or ice cream sodas at a luncheonette in town, was awarded each week to the bunk that sang the loudest. The head counselor, Micha Fogelman, served as judge. A well-built man with broad shoulders, he had a decisive air that was probably due to an incredibly authoritative voice. When he wanted silence, his command would literally pierce the air, halting all conversation in mid-sentence. Still, he needed a microphone to overcome the poor acoustics of the dining room. He would walk back and forth, stopping at various tables, his ear cocked to see which bunk was praising G-d the loudest.

After supper we went to the synagogue. The room in which we prayed was simply furnished, and designed to seat as many campers as possible. The walls were made of unpainted cinder blocks and the floor of stone. Wooden folding chairs were set up row after row right up to the bookcases that lined the back wall. Attached to the gray wall were wooden shelves upon which lay Hebrew versions of the Bible. These were given out by the counselors whenever the Torah was read.

During the week the service was not sung but recited, though great care was taken to enunciate each word properly. During the year, at home or in the synagogue, I prayed from a siddur that was about the size of a regular book. For camp, I had packed a small one. Only a bit larger than my hand, its cover was made of brown-painted metal with a few tiny rocks from the Holy Land glued into its center. It had been a gift from the rabbi of my synagogue and I treasured it greatly, running my fingers across the rocks and letting my imagination do the rest as I tried to picture the land about which I had learned so much but had never seen.

Everyone had small prayer books. Some were made of leather, others from vinyl; some had place marks, others could be completely closed by zippers. The siddur was the vehicle through which I sent my prayers heavenward. Opening it reminded me of how important a book it was to me. From constant use the pages had become rather "broken-in." A prayer book with crisp pages and unbent corners meant that the purpose for which it had been printed was still unfulfilled. Some prayers were said three times a day, others once a day, once a week or only once a year, and I remember looking forward to turning the pages upon which were printed some of the less-often-said prayers.

Every day after breakfast we would have "learning period," an hour during which all the campers studied Jewish law. The subject and format varied greatly from group to group. Beginners might be exposed to Bible stories, while the more advanced boys would be taught Talmud. During this period, wherever one looked one could see clusters of children seated around an older boy (usually a counselor). Some groups met on the porches of the various buildings, and others met beneath oaks and maples whose spreading branches offered shade from the often hot sun.

The Sabbath would be greeted by one of the counselors, who would lead us in the Friday evening service. When the cantor would begin to sing those portions that called for the congregation to join in, he did not necessarily select a melody that everyone knew. Many times he would introduce a new tune, perhaps one that he had heard from a Chasidic rebbe somewhere in Brooklyn, or from his father who had learned it in Europe, or even one that he had made up himself. Our response, halting and muted at first, would eventually grow stronger as the strains of the melody became familiar to us through repetition. What joy! What happiness! But it was only the beginning. Now we were indoors, but later on, after the Sabbath meal, the older campers would be privileged to sit outside on the porch under the starlit sky and join in as the more musically gifted counselors led us all in the Oneg Shabbos (literally, "Pleasure of the Sabbath"), the name given to a party held on the Sabbath.

I remember practically running out of the dining room

with my friends, half-dragging, half-carrying a chair and trying to position myself as near as possible to those who would be doing most of the singing. In earlier summers, I had spent many a wistful Friday night lying awake in my bed, listening as the chorus of voices on that porch wafted through the air and into the purposely opened window near the foot of my bed. But now that I was eleven, I was old enough to participate.

The melodies released the deepest emotions in me. Unlike in the city, where we were surrounded by strangers, there was no need to defensively "not care" who heard you, for the only ones who heard you were your friends, the stars, the moon, limitless night skies and, beyond all that, G-d. In my memories, the sky was always clear and studded with thousands of stars. G-d had promised Abraham that the children of Israel would be as numerous as the stars in the sky. The seeming infinity of the country sky presented a striking, crystal-clear image of what the fulfillment of that promise could mean.

We would sing for hours on end, stopping only for cookies brought out by one of the waiters. I grew to love the melodies I learned there more than any others. During the year, I would sing them for my father at the Friday night table, and as I did so the world of my inner thoughts and memories would suddenly spring alive. I was back at the camp, listening and singing, reaching out to the Lord from the depths of my spirit, reliving those magical nights.

In camp Sabbath afternoon was a time when one dwelt on matters of the spirit. From the age of eleven or twelve I studied various aspects of Jewish law by myself or with a friend once I had arisen from the Sabbath day rest. Until I reached that age, however, it was our custom in camp to go to the social hall, where, after a snack consisting of cake and soda, we would listen to stories about our people.

These stories centered around the rabbis, some from the days of the Talmud, others whose modest yet G-d-fearing lives were lived out in the hamlets of Eastern Europe: Chelm, Ropezyce, Minsk, Lomza, Slobodka, Mir—small towns, mere specks on the maps of Poland, Lithuania and Russia. What did they mean to the world at large, the Gentile world? Nothing. As a child I never realized that these places were unimportant to the rest of the world. To us they were as important as Warsaw, Cracow and Moscow. Their names had been enshrined because they had been centers of Talmudic learning and religious piety. After all, did not thousands of followers of the Gerer Rebbe journey once a year to the small village of Ger from all over Eastern Europe to see and be blessed by him? And was this not true of many other communities where well-known Jewish leaders lived?

In Eastern Europe, Jews and Gentiles led totally separate lives. The Gentile could look at his village and derive pride from the fact that his family had been there for centuries. But the Jew, always on the move, ever ready to flee, never completely at home, could rarely feel such attachment. His sense of belonging was not rooted in the meadows and pastures that surrounded him. As a despised Jew he was forbidden to own this land.

No, his strength and solace lay in the Word that had been given to him on Mount Sinai thousands of years ago, and which he carried with him wherever he went. And the tales that we heard on those Sabbath afternoons were efforts to convey the importance and timelessness of that tradition. We all sat there eager with anticipation as Moishe Pearl, a counselor, held us spellbound for hours.

Perhaps the story that made the greatest impression on me was about a talented cantor in Poland, whose beautiful voice moved worshipers to tears and to a closeness with the Almighty. One day he decided to look for a position elsewhere. Because his reputation had spread far beyond his own community, he was besieged with offers. Every congregation in Eastern Europe wanted him. Since there were so many places to choose from, the cantor traveled from town to town, investigating every offer with great care.

Finally he came to a magnificent synagogue. He was greeted enthusiastically by the president of the congregation. "This is a lovely community here. You won't find a better one in all of Europe. The acoustics in our sanctuary are marvelous; we can afford to pay you a handsome salary, and we have been living in peace with the Gentiles for over one hundred years. Moreover, we are a distinguished community. Some of the most renowned scholars in Jewish history are buried here."

At this point, the cantor, who until now had been listening with only pretended interest (after all, every congregation bragged about itself), suddenly perked up. "Who are these scholars, may I ask?" "Maimonides, Rashi, the Maharshah. To tell you the truth, there are so many in our cemetery that I simply don't know all the names." "Really," replied the cantor, "that's quite an honor. This must be a special community." In addition to being musically talented, the cantor was also a devout Jew and the religiosity of his congregants was most important to him. "I accept your offer," he said.

A few weeks later the cantor arrived with his family. After unloading their belongings in their new house, the cantor set out for the synagogue. It was late afternoon and he wanted to meet some of the people, who, he assumed, were by now finished with the day's work and studying the Talmud. Upon entering he found the synagogue totally deserted. He was about to leave when he heard the sound of a chair scraping behind a door near the front of the synagogue, a little to the left of the Holy Ark. Curious, he knocked twice, softly. "Come in," answered a quavering voice. The cantor entered and found himself face to face with a bespectacled, wizened old man of slender build. The man was seated facing him, behind a rickety-looking wooden table. Various seforim (holy books) were strewn about the table in a manner suggesting that their user relied on them heavily and often. "What can I do for you, fellow Jew?" he asked. "I'm your new cantor. Where is everybody?" The old man gave the cantor a scornful look and laughed mirthlessly before responding in a voice heavily tinged with sarcasm: "I imagine they're where they always are—in the tavern. I'm the only one that still studies the holy books. The rest of them . . ." His voice trailed off. The cantor asked the man for directions to the tavern, thanked him and hurried off.

Upon arriving there he looked around for the president, finally spotting him seated at a table with a group of other congregants, whom the cantor had also met before. They were laughing loudly and drinking, and, in general, acting in a manner that was improper for a G-d-fearing Jew and keeper of the commandments. The cantor angrily confronted the president: "What kind of a community is this? I walk into the synagogue and I find one man studying there. The rest of you are here, drinking and carousing. You told me that this was a distinguished community. You said that some of our greatest scholars were buried here. Now I see that you have deceived me and made a fool of me."

The president looked at him and said, "Calm down, my man, calm down. It's true that I said 'distinguished,' but who can judge the meaning of such a word? What one man considers distinguished, another does not. As to my state-

126

ment about the scholars who are buried here, I told you the truth. You simply failed to grasp it. When I said these men are buried here, I meant that nobody studies their writings any more. As you can see, my congregants are not interested in Maimonides or Rashi and so for all practical purposes they might as well be dead and buried."

After Moishe had told this story, he would pause for a moment or two to allow the full effect of his words to sink in. Then he would say something like "The majesty and splendor of the Torah exist only so long as the children of Israel study and follow its teachings. And it is the duty of each and every one of you to see that the flame of learning is never extinguished. That is the true purpose for which we were put on this earth." His closing speech was hardly necessary for most of us, for we had been taught from our earliest years that this was what mattered. Camp Tikvath Shalom was but a continuation of my way of life. Though I might play ball, go on overnight hikes, watch movies and pursue hobbies such as lanyard-making, these were merely temporary concessions to the understandable temptations of childhood. They were not what was important in life.

Not everything in camp was joyous. The saddest holiday of the year, the Ninth of Ab, came during the summer months. This was the date on which the Holy Temple in Jerusalem had been destroyed. Both Temples built by the Jews burned to the ground on that day. The First Temple had been laid waste by the Babylonians in 586 B.C.E. and the Second by the Romans in 70 C.E. This catastrophe marked the end of Jewish independence and the beginning of their exile and dispersion throughout the world. Curiously enough, the last Jew to leave Spain after the expulsion order in 1492 left on Tisha baAb (as it is called in Hebrew).

Actually, Tisha baAb was the last day of a three-week period of mourning which began on the day that the Babylonians first breached the walls of Jerusalem. The tragic nature of this event pervaded every aspect of camp life. During this three-week period, no movies were shown nor were haircuts permitted. Beginning on the ninth-from-last day, the swimming pool was closed to everyone but the youngest campers. We could not buy or wear new clothing during those nine days, nor could we wash our dirty clothing —we simply left it in our laundry bags until after the mourning period. In addition, no meat was served except on the Sabbath. The only occasion on which it was permissible to eat meat was when someone in the camp (usually an older boy or counselor) had completed a portion of the Talmud. When that happened, the young man would present a learned discourse on the last section of what he had learned for about forty-five minutes to the entire camp. After that, everyone was allowed to eat meat, for by virtue of that presentation the meal had become one commemorating the fulfillment of a mitzvah and that happy event took precedence over even the mourning period.

Finally, after each meal, the saying of grace was preceded by the chanting of the 137th Psalm:

By the rivers of Babylon, there we sat and wept as we recalled Zion.

We hung our harps in the midst of the willows.

There those that carried us off in captivity forced us to sing,

And those who wasted us, compelled us to be happy, saying: "Sing for us a song of Zion."

These were my ancestors. Their sorrow was mine. They had wept by the rivers of Babylon, in the ghettos of Europe and the Near East, and in the death camps. Their fate was ours, our sorrow a mirror-image of their vanished dreams. Had the Nazis learned from the Babylonians when they created symphony orchestras made up of concentration camp inmates and commanded them to sing and be happy?

How shall we sing the Lord's song on strange soil?

If I forget thee, O Jerusalem, let my right hand fail me.

Let my tongue cleave to the roof of my mouth if I do not remember thee,

If I do not prefer Jerusalem above my chief joy.

On the Ninth of Ab, the entire camp participated in a collective outpouring of grief. Beginning with the night before Tisha baAb it was forbidden to eat or drink anything. We would have our last full meal sometime in the late afternoon. Then, as evening fell, I and all the other campers walked back to our bunks, where the counselors gave each camper a cold hard-boiled egg to eat. The egg had been dipped lightly into ashes to commemorate the destruction of the Temple. By the time we finished it was already dusk and it would be twenty-four hours before we could eat again.

Everyone headed for the social hall, where special arrangements had been made so that the fast could be properly observed. The benches had been turned over on their sides, for as a sign of mourning no one was allowed to sit on anything higher than a small stool. As a result we needed far more leg room and could therefore not worship in the small synagogue where we generally prayed. Some people had taken wooden soda boxes from the counter to sit on, and others were sitting on the floor, their backs propped against the walls of the building. Everyone was wearing sneakers, since, as a symbol of mourning, it was not permissible to wear shoes made of leather.

As I walked in, I was given a copy of the Book of Lamentations by someone standing at the door. When everyone was seated, Rabbi Berezin, the owner of the camp, began reading from the Book with a weeping intonation. Even if one could not comprehend the meaning of a single word, there was no mistaking the grief in the rabbi's voice. The front of the Holy Ark, behind which lay the Holy Scrolls, was bare, its wooden doors that opened out uncovered for the first and only time in the year. The velvet curtain had been removed to emphasize the sadness of the occasion. The pervasiveness of the gloom that gripped us all was highlighted by the fact that only a few lights were on in the large hall, barely enough to read by.

We sat for several hours in this manner. Different people took turns reading, but each one's voice sounded almost identical to me, for they were all chanting about the same tragedy: Our Temple was no more; it had been gone for two thousand years, and even though we had a country now, no Temple had yet been built there, since the Messiah had not come. Instead, all that was left was one wall, the "Wailing Wall" as it was named, and even that was denied us, for the Jordanians refused to allow the Jews access to it.

It seemed to me as though the era of the Temple had been but a short time ago. The rituals we performed effectively prevented us from treating this day as though it were a relic of the ancient past. I remember on one occasion squirming uncomfortably in the small space that I had secured in a corner of the room and complaining to my counselor. "You feel uncomfortable?" he said harshly. "Think of what it must have been like for Bnai Yisroel [Children of Israel] when they saw the holiest place in the whole land burning to the ground." He had been too sharp with me, but his sincerity could not be questioned. I saw tears in his eyes, and though I sulked for the remainder of the night, I felt shamed.

130

Even after services had ended, our mourning continued. We went to sleep without any of the horseplay that usually accompanied our counselor's efforts to get us to bed. Moreover, since we were not supposed to feel comfortable in the least, we slept without pillows that night. I always had difficulty falling asleep on Tisha baAb night. I would lie awake thinking about the importance of the occasion. Most of the time, though, I was unable to sustain the level of emotion that had taken hold of me earlier in the evening, when I had been a part of a large group of supplicants to the Almighty.

The first part of the next day was virtually a repetition of the previous evening. Again we went to the social hall, but by now the first pangs of hunger were beginning to strike me. According to Jewish law, one was not required to fast the whole day until one had reached the age of thirteen, but that never deterred me or any of my friends from trying. It was, in our religious world, a sign of manhood to be able to go an entire day without eating or drinking. After all, among those who were of age, only people who were ill were allowed to eat on Tisha baAb. It was forbidden to say even "Good morning," and we had been taught that if someone unaware of that law approached us on that day with a greeting, we should respond for the sake of politeness but only in a low tone of voice. Even phylacteries and prayer shawls were not worn on Tisha baAb, because they were considered symbols of beauty.

Beginning at noon, we were no longer required to sit on boxes or on the floor. By early afternoon, services were usually over and we were free to go outside. It always seemed hotter on Tisha baAb than at any other time during the summer. Once we left the social hall for the outdoors, the importance of the fast began rapidly dissipating. My friends and I sat around talking about what we would eat if we could. "I'd love a big ice cream soda with nuts, chocolate syrup and a big maraschino cherry on top," said one boy. "I'll have a banana sundae!" shouted another. And invariably someone else, whose resistance might have been a bit weaker than the rest, would complain, "Hey, stop it, you guys. You're making me nauseous."

Tiring of this after a while, we would walk around the camp. There was little else to do, for ball playing was strictly forbidden on this day. Besides, we felt too weak for such exertions. Finally, the sun would begin its long descent into the distance, gradually disappearing over the hills. In another hour or so we would eat our first meal of the day, famished and certain that it was the best food we had ever tasted. The Temple had actually been set ablaze on the Ninth of Ab, but the fire continued burning through the night and into the next day. Thus no one was permitted to eat meat, bathe or shave until noon of the following day. Yet when that time came, joyousness swept through the camp quickly, contrasting sharply with the atmosphere of the previous day. In the dining room, Hillel Zimmerman, one of the counselors, would strike up a quick happy tune on his accordion and everyone would join in singing and clapping hands. The time of mourning was passed. Life went on.

Though we were expected to pray a good deal, recite blessings when we ate, study the Holy writings and fastidiously observe the Sabbath and other holidays, we were still children in every other way. We might pout if not chosen for a punchball game, balk at eating our carrots and, as a practical joke, place a cup of water over the door to the bunk so that it would fall on the counselor's head when he entered.

Although my upbringing was religious, there were still gaps here and there. Light of Abraham Yeshiva did not, for instance, have school on Sunday, and that in itself was a strong indicator of how "modern" a yeshiva it was. The majority of the boys at Camp Tikvath Shalom came from yeshivas in Brooklyn which considered Sunday to be like any other day. Partly because of this extra day and partly because it symbolized a philosophy that paid less attention to what was happening in the world around it, my fellow campers were usually more advanced in the study of the Talmud. In response, I tried hard to catch up, and those efforts may in turn have accounted in some measure for the success I had in studying Talmud at Light of Abraham during the year.

There was a bungalow colony next door named Shady Hill. Only irreligious Jews went there, and for us the colony was strictly off limits. It had a small store where one could buy candy, soda, fruits and vegetables, and one day I and two of my bunkmates left the bunk on some pretext and headed over to the line of trees that separated the camp from the colony. We approached the area, clambered over a small rise in the ground, through the thick underbrush, and were in.

We walked over to some elderly people who were sunning themselves on beach chairs. "Where's the candy store?" I asked. A bare-chested man with a blue captain's hat and dark-green sunglasses pointed lazily in the direction of a small bungalow whose front was adorned with a large sign that read "COCA-COLA," and a smaller one beneath that proclaimed, "BORDEN'S ICE CREAM." "Right over there, kids." We hurried over, for we did not want to be missed by the camp. The store itself was rather nondescript. It was, however, distinguished by one feature absent from Camp Tikvath

Shalom—a pinball machine. A girl about my age was playing it and seemed totally oblivious to our presence.

I walked over and asked if we could play the machine. "Sure," she said, "go ahead, but remember, just one game." She had long black braids and a soft face, with gentle features and the largest, almond-shaped, brown eyes I had ever seen. "Okay," I said, "just one game." I called over my friends and we wound up sharing that one game, each of us taking turns at hitting the little silver ball with the plunger. The whole thing took three minutes. As we were leaving I could not resist calling over my shoulder to the girl, who was by now back at the machine, "We'll be back." "Any time," she said, flashing me a quick smile. We got back safely. No one had noticed our absence.

Encouraged, I began going over there myself whenever I had a chance. I became friendly with the girl. Her name was Susie, and she attended a public school somewhere in the Bronx. Susie was a good listener, warm and sympathetic, and when she laughed, it was as though a breath of fresh air had entered the store. By my fifth visit we were holding hands and sharing ice cream.

Then, disaster. It was a rainy afternoon. I was sitting with Susie by the fountain on the little red revolving stool, when Menachem Zachs, my counselor, suddenly pushed open the screen door and walked in. "Who told you you could leave camp grounds?" he thundered. "Do you know I've been looking all over for you for the last half-hour!" Had I been gone that long? "If not for David [one of the boys who had accompanied me on our first trip], I still wouldn't know where you were. C'mon, we're going back right now." Menachem propelled me out the door. I was terrified. What would he do now? Would he report me to Rabbi Berezin? And what would be my fate then? I began pleading with him. "Please don't get me in trouble. I'll never do it again. I promise, Menachem. *Please?*" Menachem looked at me briefly. When he saw the terror in my eyes, his own expression softened somewhat. "We'll see when we get back to the bunk."

When we got back, Menachem ordered everyone out of the bunk. "Sit down, Willy," he said. "I'm not going to give you a long speech. You know what you did wrong. I'm just warning you that if I ever catch you off camp grounds *and especially with a girl,* you're going right to Rabbi Berezin. Is that clear?" he said, glowering. "Yes, Menachem," I murmured contritely. "All right, you can go outside now."

I went out and sat on the porch. "Especially with a girl." There was no mistaking the emphasis in Menachem's words.

My yeshiva was coed. All our classes were held with boys and girls in the same room (the practice has since been changed). I had never thought there was anything particularly wrong with talking to girls. On the other hand, the counselors and campers at Camp Tikvath Shalom were more Orthodox than most of the people at the Light of Abraham Yeshiva and felt that truly religious boys did not associate with girls. Who was right—my father, who never really expressed any negative views on the subject, my teachers and the principal at the yeshiva, or Menachem and the people at the camp? It was a perplexing issue for a twelve-year-old. Yet I knew from all sorts of little comments made and not made that this was a sensitive area—the less said the better. And so I stifled my feelings and never again brought up the subject as long as I was in camp. As for Susie, I never saw her again.

The summer before I entered high school was my last one as a camper at Camp Tikvath Shalom. My counselor was

135

Daniel Zimet, a student in the Gates of Israel Yeshiva, an institution approximately two hundred miles from New York and universally recognized as belonging to the "Ivy League" of such schools. Daniel exemplified everything that I wanted to be. His soft voice and gentle demeanor made him perhaps the most loved person in the camp. As a Talmudic scholar, he was brilliant. Everyone wanted to be in his learning group. He could communicate an idea better than anyone I knew, and my mind, questing as it was, responded eagerly. Besides, Daniel could hit a baseball literally out of sight and was acknowledged as the fastest swimmer in the camp.

Daniel and I began studying the Talmud together on Sabbath afternoons for an hour or so before Mincha (the afternoon service). He appeared to be genuinely interested in me, and I redoubled my efforts to please him during those sessions. One day Daniel said, "Willy, have you ever thought about going to the Gates of Israel Yeshiva? It is one of the most famous in the world." I said nothing, too surprised to answer. Daniel continued: "You would live in the Yeshiva and be part of a community of B'nai Torah [literally, 'Sons of the Torah']. It's something to think about. When I made the decision to go to study at the Yeshiva, I took a long time, too. It was the smartest choice of my life."

I spent about a week mulling over the idea, thinking about what it would be like to leave my home and my friends. To explain what Daniel's idea meant to me, perhaps I should start from the beginning.

After the destruction of the Second Temple, the Jews were expelled from Palestine and dispersed throughout the Roman Empire. Although many Jews were lost to the community, the Jewish people continued to exist as a distinct entity throughout the world. Perhaps the most important reason for this survival was the Talmud. By interpreting and expanding upon the Five Books of Moses, the Talmud was assured of a continuing role as a living doctrine to be studied and adhered to. It dealt not only with laws and their justifications, but also with ethics and morals. Moreover, it touched upon medicine, hygiene, government, mathematics and business.

The Talmud was traditionally studied in the yeshiva. Communities were often measured in terms of how good their yeshivas were. As time passed, the centers of influence moved from the Babylonian academies to Northern Africa and Europe. By the thirteenth century, wherever significant numbers of Jews were living, yeshivas had been established.

In the eighteenth century, European Jewry was emancipated from many social and economic restrictions that had hampered it throughout the centuries. Numerous Jews took advantage of the new opportunities that now awaited them in the outside world. At the same time, however, even larger numbers remained committed to their traditional beliefs and practices. This was most true of Jews in Russia, Lithuania, Poland and other parts of Eastern Europe, where innumerable yeshivas continued to attract thousands upon thousands of students each year.

With the outbreak of World War II, millions of Jews were slaughtered. Among those fortunate enough to have left Eastern Europe before it was too late, or to have survived the Holocaust, were the leaders of numerous yeshivas. They came to the United States and founded institutions, or academies, modeled after their European predecessors. While the majority of such yeshivas were set up in the New York City area, where the largest number of Orthodox Jews lived, a few were also built in other parts of the United States.

137

The Gates of Israel Yeshiva had originally been situated in Lithuania and had a long and venerable tradition. In going there (if they decided to accept me), I would become a part of that history. My acute awareness of the significance of the yeshiva spurred on my decision. I had been interested in the Talmud for several years, far longer than the average boy my age, and I had already shown a considerable degree of aptitude in that subject. Added to this were my father's keen desire to have me become a "talmid chachem" and Daniel's encouragement.

The next visiting day I spoke with my parents of my wish to attend the Yeshiva. "Daddy," I said, "I want to go study in the Gates of Israel Yeshiva." "Why do you want to go?" he asked. I told him about Daniel, whom I so greatly admired. "Daniel says it's a really fine place, one where I could develop into a real talmid chachem." "But are you sure you want to be so far away from home?" my father asked. In reality, the idea of going to a place two hundred miles from home when I had rarely even been outside New York State held a great attraction for me, but I knew better than to say *that.* I looked my father squarely in the eye and said: "Daddy, I want to be a mensch." Now "mensch" is a Yiddish expression which, translated loosely, means a person of substance or consequence. My father, convinced that I was serious, gave his consent.

At the end of summer, I came home from camp, unpacked and then immediately repacked for the Gates of Israel.

By the time I arrived in

the city where the Yeshiva was situated, I was nearly bursting from nervousness and anticipation. I hailed a cab and gave the driver the address. On the way, I kept up a steady chatter of conversation, trying in this manner to stave off my anxiety. Finally, we arrived. I took my suitcases out of the trunk of the cab with the help of the driver and paid him. As the cab left, I took stock of my surroundings.

The street was lined with one- and two-family houses whose front lawns were neatly manicured. Small, black-painted lamp posts were spaced at intervals along the block, and large trees gave the area a somewhat rustic appearance. Directly in front of me was a two-story red-brick building with three square-shaped, granite pillars rising up to the roof. On top was a Star of David, also made of granite. The words "Gates of Israel" were carved in Hebrew letters into the front wall.

I lifted my bags, walked through the two red-brick gate-posts and up the concrete walk that led to the entrance. I had not gone more than a half-dozen steps when the front door opened and two young men about nineteen or twenty emerged. "Wait a minute, we'll help you," shouted one of them. As they drew near, I saw that they were dressed in the manner customary for yeshiva students: large black yarmulkes, plain pants and jackets, white shirts open at the collar, with woolen fringes hanging down from the waist on both sides.

"Sholem aleichem [Peace be unto you]," said one of the boys, extending a pale white hand. "Aleichem sholem [Unto you be peace]," I answered in the traditional manner, inverting the words. "Sholem aleichem," said the second youth, and again I responded accordingly. Each took one suitcase, leaving me to carry the small shopping bag into which, at the last minute, my mother had put an extra pair of pajamas and a heavy woolen sweater.

As we walked into the building, I was struck by its austerity. Plain walls without any decorations, painted dark gray and white. The bare floor was beige in color and looked rather worn. We went up a flight of stairs to the second floor, where the high school dormitory was located. The first floor, I was to learn shortly, was reserved for the Beis haMedrash (House of Study), for classroom space and for administrative offices. My new acquaintances dropped off the suitcases before an open door through which I could see another young man seated near the entrance at a small, bare wooden table. A wildly flickering fluorescent lamp rested on its scratched top.

"Please come in," he said, simultaneously extending his hand and saying, "Sholem aleichem. I'm Motti Kanowitz and I'll be your dormitory counselor. Any problems, you come to me," he finished. I told him my name, whereupon he returned to his desk and, removing a thick sheaf of papers from the desk drawer, looked through them, eventually pulling one out. "Helmreich, eh? Okay, let's see—you're in room 18, down the hall and to your right." I thanked him and, picking up my bags once more, made my way to my room.

The door was slightly ajar, and as I pushed it open, I saw a slender, dark-haired youth about my age, sitting on a chair, reading a copy of *Mesillath Yesharim*, the great book of ethics and morals written in the eighteenth century by Rabbi Moshe Chaim Luzzatto. Upon seeing me, he jumped up and greeted me enthusiastically. His name was Yehuda Avineri and he was an Israeli. Yehuda had come here, I learned, because his late father, may he rest in peace, had been a student at the same Lithuanian seminary that the founder of the Gates of Israel Yeshiva had attended, and it had been his father's dying wish that his son journey to America and attend his friend's yeshiva.

I looked around at the room that would be my home for the next year at least. It was simply, almost spartanly furnished, with two double-decker beds, four dressers, a couple of chairs and a few closets. A washbasin protruded from the wall, which was slightly cracked and beginning to peel. I took the three remaining empty dresser drawers and began putting my things inside them.

Suddenly Yehuda exclaimed: "Hey, you'd better not let anybody see that." "See what?" I asked. "That," he replied, pointing to my blue transistor radio. It had been a Bar Mitzvah present from one of my cousins. By now it was ready to fall apart, and I had periodically Scotch-taped the two parts of the plastic cover together. I treasured it greatly. "What's wrong with having a radio?" "It's against the Yeshiva rules," said Yehuda. "The Yeshiva feels there's a lot of shtuss [nonsense] on the radio these days—you know, rock 'n' roll and the like—and besides, it takes away from the study of the Torah." Then, seeing the look of astonishment on my face, Yehuda went on: "Don't worry. It's not so bad. In a few weeks at the most you'll begin to understand what the Yeshiva is trying to accomplish and then these rules won't seem so strange to you."

At this point, my two other roommates walked in and introduced themselves. One was from a small town in Pennsylvania. Unlike Yehuda, he was a first-year student in the Yeshiva. Almost six feet tall with a muscular build, he would have looked very much at home on any high school football team. But this was deceptive. Yitzchak Schaeffer turned out to be one of the most studious boys in the Yeshiva.

The second fellow was Michael Wasserman. Born in Siberia, where his parents had fled from Hitler's onslaught, he had spent his childhood years in Los Angeles. His father, a wealthy businessman, was a good friend of the Yeshiva's executive director, Rabbi Alter. Michael was dressed in an orange and blue shirt and a tight pair of chinos and did not appear to be serious at all. Within a few months, though, he became almost fanatical in his devotion both to the study of the Talmud and to the religious practices that absorbed us.

There were about three hundred students in the high school and advanced divisions. Over supper I met a number of other boys and discovered that they came from every part of the country: Tennessee, Arizona, Florida, Connecticut, Illinois, Michigan and many other states. They came from small towns and large metropolises. Some were from observant homes and others were not, but they shared one common bond: the quest for a better understanding and appreciation of their ancient faith, a desire to enrich both their spiritual and intellectual lives.

We spent half the night talking to each other, exchanging backgrounds and experiences. In addition to the regulation against owning a radio, attending movies was forbidden, as was socializing with members of the opposite sex. I gave little thought to these restrictions at the time, for I was determined not to let anything interfere with the romantic image of the Yeshiva that my mind had created.

The next morning at 7 A.M., we were all wakened by the sound of someone shouting in Yiddish in the halls of the dormitory: "Shteht oif, shteht oif, l'avoidas haBoiray! Shteht oif, shteht oif, l'avoidas haBoiray!" ("Wake up, wake up, to do the work of the Creator! Wake up, wake up, to do the work of the Creator!") The voice, I discovered later, belonged to one of the students, who had assumed the responsibility for waking everyone. The room was still dark as I reached over to the chair beside the bed, donned my skullcap, stumbled out of bed to wash my hands ritually, and began reciting the prayer said upon awakening: "I thank Thee, O Lord, who has mercifully returned my soul to me; Thy faith in me is great."

We dressed quickly and in silence. It was considered inappropriate to engage in extended conversation with others before one had prayed to the Almighty. As I emerged into the hallway, I could see and hear the doors to other rooms opening, their occupants stepping outside to join the ever-growing stream of worshipers as they filed down the stairs to the Beis haMedrash, which was also our synagogue, for the morning service.

The Beis haMedrash accommodated about 150 persons. About thirty wooden tables were arranged one behind the other, with room for four or five boys at each table. In the center of the room stood a square table over which was draped a dark-blue velvet cover with a yellow Star of David in its center. This was where the Torah was placed on the days when portions of it were read. In the front of the room was the Holy Ark, where the Torah lay when not in use. On each side of the Ark were three wooden shtenders, or lecterns, about four and a half feet high, on which to put reading matter, with a chair behind each one. These were reserved for the six rabbis who taught in our division. There

143

was a larger Beis haMedrash down the hall for older and more advanced students.

I found a seat near the back of the room and began putting on my tefillin. Glancing about, I was struck by how slowly many of the boys were performing this act. When, in earlier years, I had accompanied my father to synagogue on weekday mornings in New York, the congregants had always slipped on their tefillin quickly, almost as though it were a race. But then, I suddenly realized, they had to go to work in the morning and attending synagogue was, in terms of time, quite a sacrifice for them. Here, however, it was different. No one was in a hurry. There were no trains to catch, no clocks to punch and no earthly jobs to be done. It would be inexcusable in this environment to rush through one's prayers, not to dwell on the words themselves as long as one felt necessary.

Removing the cover, I placed the small black box squarely on my bicep so that when my arm hung at my side it would be directly opposite my heart. This was in keeping with the spirit of the passage in Deuteronomy 11:18: "And ye shall put My words upon your hearts." I then said the blessing: "Blessed art Thou, Lord our G-d, King of the Universe, who has sanctified us with His commandments and commanded us to put on tefillin." Next, I tightened the box by pulling on the black strap and winding it around my arm seven times. The remaining length of strap I wound around the palm of my hand.

Having completed this portion of the ritual, I uncovered the other black box and placed it on my head above the forehead, making certain that the lowest point of the box was not below the hairline. A head strap looped through the box encircled my head and two black straps hung down the back.

As I put this on, I recited the blessing: "Blessed art Thou, Lord our G-d, King of the Universe, who has sanctified us with His commandments and commanded us concerning the mitzvah of tefillin." Once I was certain that the tefillin were securely in place on my head, I uttered the words "Blessed be He whose glorious majesty is forever and ever." I was now ready for the last step.

I unwrapped the strap from the palm of my hand and rewound it around my fingers and hand in such a manner as to spell out the holy name "Shaddai." While doing this I quoted aloud the passage from Hosea 2:21–22:

I will betroth you to Myself forever;

I will betroth you to Myself in righteousness and in justice, in kindness and in mercy.

I will betroth you to Myself in faithfulness and you shall know the Lord.

"Yes," I thought, "I've surely done that in coming here." Already, then, I had the feeling deep inside me that this had been a divinely inspired decision—to submit myself to the will of the Lord, and to be a servant in His employ.

We began saying the prayers very carefully, each word measured out and reflected upon. Though the prayers were the same as those I had always recited, I had never before witnessed such intensity and fervor around me. I noticed that I was praying faster than most of the others. Not wanting to feel different, I began to slow down my pace somewhat, saying the prayers in a fashion similar to the others', with perhaps a greater show of devotion than I actually felt.

At one point in the service there was a pause for about ten seconds, and then, suddenly, came the words, first from one part of the large room, then from another, first one voice, then a second, and finally the entire congregation, each person with his hand covering his eyes: "Hear, O Israel, the Lord is our G-d, the Lord is One!" As I swayed back and forth in my seat, I was seized by a feeling of closeness to G-d, of emotional gratification and of a bond between myself and those seated around me. This prayer was called the Shema (literally, "hear"). Down through the ages, numberless Jews who had died in the name of the faith had left this world with that phrase on their lips.

No matter how slowly I prayed, I still finished ahead of the rabbis seated in the front. Their eyes were shut tight, their prayer shawls over their heads, as they articulated the words. Everyone, including the cantor, a young boy, waited, as a sign of respect, until they were done. Then the cantor would finish the last few words of the prayer, "I am the Lord your G-d, true and firm."

The entire service lasted almost an hour. Afterward everyone went into the communal dining room for breakfast. We washed our hands with a large tin cup in the manner prescribed by law. I sat down on a wooden bench at one of the long tables in the room, broke off a piece of bread, salted it and then said: "Blessed art Thou, Lord our G-d, King of the Universe, who brings forth bread from the earth."

I was seated with the new boys. For the most part, our conversation that first day dealt with mundane matters. As time passed, however, and I became immersed in yeshiva life, I would begin making a conscious effort to spend as much time as possible talking about matters pertaining to the Talmud, and to Judaism in general. At the conclusion of the morning meal we said grace together and headed back to the House of Study to begin doing "the work of the Creator."

I had been told that my rebbe, or teacher, would be Rav

Landau, and so, upon walking into the Beis haMedrash, I asked for him. "Right there," said a boy seated at a table, his Gemara in front of him. Following his pointing finger, I saw a medium-sized, round-shaped figure standing at a shtender, talking animatedly with a youth about my age. I approached carefully, for even from a distance it was obvious that they were "talking in learning," and I did not wish to interrupt them. I stood off to the side for a few moments and waited to be acknowledged. I knew that Rav Landau had already seen me out of the corner of his eye and so I was not surprised when, after a short time, he turned to me with an expectant look.

"I'm Naftoli Helmreich," I said, pausing and hoping he would recognize my name. "Of course," he said, shaking my hand warmly, "Daniel told me about you. Sholem aleichem." I felt relieved and instantly comfortable. His white complexion was emphasized by a curly black untrimmed beard, which literally surrounded his face. A pair of soft large brown eyes looked out from beneath a set of long pencil-thin eyebrows. A large black hat was perched on his head. It was tilted back at a slight angle to reveal the beginnings of a thick mass of curly black hair. He appeared to be in his early thirties.

"Come, Naftoli, let me introduce you to your chavrusah [learning partner]." We walked over to where a red-cheeked, cherubic-looking boy was sitting. "Zevulun, this is Naftoli. He'll be your chavrusah." Zevulun greeted me cordially but shyly. He was from Canada and this was his first time away from home. Though he was a year younger than I, he had been studying Gamara since the fourth grade and was therefore quite advanced for his years. "Boys, I want you to try to make a 'leining' on the first part of the page here," said Rav Landau, placing a stubby finger near the top,

147

on the left-hand side of Zevulun's Gemara.

A "leining" meant trying to understand a portion of the Talmud before it was taught in class. The idea was that by struggling to understand the arguments of the rabbis and the logic used to support them, one would eventually acquire the ability to learn on one's own, even when no rebbe was present. This was one reason why it was important to have a good learning partner. No one really watched over us while we studied. True, the rebbes would notice if someone constantly fooled around, but, generally speaking, we were expected to be seriously involved on our own. Naturally, everyone felt tempted at times to talk about other matters, and as a result it was crucial to have a chavrusah who was not too much inclined in this direction.

Ideal study partners were boys whose level of Talmudic understanding was roughly equal. If one boy was far superior to the other, then that boy's progress would be impeded by the need to explain everything to the less informed one. Conversely, the less advanced student would generally perceive that he was holding back the other and might therefore refrain from asking necessary questions about that which he did not understand.

Zevulun and I were well suited to each other. Our level of understanding was about equal (actually, he was a bit better) and we complemented each other perfectly in terms of personality. This in turn was reflected in our method of study. For example, Zevulun tended to be methodical, trying to understand each step in the argument before proceeding to the next one, while I, on the other hand, looked for hidden reasons or insights, sometimes ignoring the details and going by intuition. In reality, both were necessary for a full appreciation of the depth and range of the Talmud. This was, however, our first day and so we knew nothing

148

about each other. Not until weeks later did these distinct characteristics become apparent.

Each year, the entire Yeshiva would select one particular tractate of the Talmud to study. That year it was the one known as *Vows*. In ancient times it was common practice to make vows. A person might make a vow in anger or he might deny himself certain pleasures through the making of a vow. Although the Talmud observes at one point that the rabbis generally disapproved of the idea, they did not expressly forbid it. Over the years certain procedures developed concerning the proper way to make a vow, and the tractate of *Vows* was devoted to a discussion of, among other things, how these vows were to be articulated. It also dealt with partners in the ownership of property who made vows, how one set time limits in the making of vows, how vows could be annulled and so on.

The subject was more or less new to me, though I knew about it in a general way. It frequently occurred that in the study of one portion of the Talmud a proof might be brought to bear on a certain issue by quoting from another volume of the Talmud. Thus, in learning other tractates, I had come across references to the tractate of *Vows*. Still, nothing compared with the in-depth manner in which the subject would now be covered.

Zevulun and I spent the next hour and a half trying to make sense of what was being said, and as we argued back and forth, I felt as though I had entered another country, for all around me boys were doing the exact same thing. And if I had looked, I would probably have seen my own happiness reflected in the joyful expressions on their faces as they talked, listened and studied in the singsong melody familiar to Talmudic scholars the world over. This was what I had come here for!

At 11 A.M. all the boys left the House of Study for class. Zevulun and I had done a fairly good job, I thought, of preparing for what was to be our first formal learning experience at the Yeshiva. I had just sat down in the classroom with some of the other boys when Rav Landau entered. All conversation ceased immediately. The only sound that could be heard was the scraping of chairs as everyone stood up. We would do this, as a sign of deference when he entered, every day for the remainder of the year, just as we would always refer to the rabbis there in the third person.

"Sit, sit," said Rav Landau, placing his large bound copy of the tractate of *Vows* on the desk in front of him. I noticed that the pages were yellowed with age, their jagged edges indicative of heavy use by their owner. "Nu, who knows the Gemara? Who wants to start reading first?" Several hands shot up around the room. "Okay, Yossi, you start," said the rebbe, motioning to a lanky, bespectacled youth with close-cropped, sandy hair sitting in the back.

Yossi began reading, first saying the words in the original, then translating into English. Of the approximately twenty-five boys in the class, a good number understood and spoke Yiddish, but except in two of the older rabbis' classes, the Talmud was explained in English. This in itself was something of a concession to the times and reflected the fact that most of our rabbis, while they were successful carriers of the Orthodox tradition, had been raised in an American milieu.

"What does Rav Ashi mean here, Yossi?" asked Rav Landau. Yossi repeated his translation. "But what is the meaning *behind* those words?" asked Rav Landau. Everyone was silent, trying to guess what the rebbe was driving at. It was hardly surprising that we should become bogged down right at the beginning, for each word in the Talmud was so important. One could not simply read it as one might a book.

Every phrase had to be carefully evaluated both in terms of the words themselves and with regard to the order in which they appeared.

Eventually, with the help of the rebbe we figured out what Rav Ashi meant, discovering at the same time that what had at first seemed obvious was not, that what looked like a simple statement was fraught with difficulties. As the discussion moved on, boys would quote from other books in the Talmud, bringing proofs for and against what was being said here.

"But it's a contradiction," said one boy.

"No, it's not!" retorted another.

"Why not?" said the first.

"Because the two cases are different."

"How?" asked the other.

Pretty soon the entire room reverberated with the sound of voices, each clamoring for Rav Landau's attention, all trying to be heard. The two protagonists had by now acquired allies among the other boys. Finally, Rav Landau said, "All right, boys; enough, enough! Let's look at it again." And he would painstakingly review the line that was giving everyone so much trouble.

Sometimes it was a question of where the sentence ended; at other times it was a matter of which one of several definitions to apply to a word. Clearly, the rebbe was far more knowledgeable than we were, yet he played down his own erudition. He was always trying to get us to figure out the answer on our own and came to our aid only when we seemed hopelessly lost. Moreover, I found that he often imputed greater wisdom to us than we had. To make an original point in class, to ask an incisive question, was regarded as one of the highest achievements, and whenever that happened to me, I would glow.

Many times, however, it only seemed to occur. A boy would start to say something and Rav Landau would say, "You mean that such and such cannot be so because it would create a problem in the case discussed last week?" Everyone immediately grasped, from the rebbe's enthusiastic expression and tone, that this was an important point, yet it may not have been what the boy was trying to say. It became difficult, under such circumstances, to deny having meant what the rebbe thought you said. Sometimes the boy would say, "Yes, this is what I meant," and the rebbe would then explain the idea to the rest of the class. "What Binyomin is trying to bring out here is that . . ." At other times, especially among the better students, who were more sure of themselves and less afraid of being wrong, the boy would say, "No, that was not the intention of my words."

Rav Landau understood each boy in the class. He sensed which ones needed coaxing and encouragement to improve and which ones required an occasional scolding. Moreover, he took a genuine interest in each boy and by virtue of the gentleness of his personality won over virtually everyone who had contact with him.

Although much of what we studied dealt with legalities and demanded a rigorous application of the principles of logic, a tremendous amount of space in the Talmud was devoted to topics whose scope and diversity never ceased to amaze me. Among these were honoring the aged, cheating, compassion, how to say the blessings, love, the treatment of animals, a father's responsibilities, trespassing, drunkenness, the Sabbath, behavior toward orphans, murder, choosing a mate, Passover and many, many other subjects.

Even *Vows,* one of the more technical sections of the Talmud, was replete with aphorisms, moral insights and principles of daily conduct. For example, there was the story of Rabbi Helbo, who became ill, whereupon Rabbi Kahana publicly announced: "Rabbi Helbo is sick." (*Vows,* 40a, Babylonian Edition.) Yet no one came to visit him. As a result, Rabbi Kahana admonished the people by telling them the story of how the great Rabbi Akiba visited an ill disciple of his, and subsequent to that visit the disciple recovered. Following that, Rabbi Akiba proclaimed that "he who fails to visit the sick, it is as though he has shed blood."

The message was clear, and I, who had been brought up to revere and love the Torah, felt reassured by this and other expressions of human concern. The Talmud's wisdom was demonstrated to me not only through brilliant arguments but also by tales of the various rabbis' lives. There was a story in the book of *Vows* about a man who came to Rabbi Judah, the son of Shalom, to annul a vow. "What did you swear not to do?" asked Rabbi Judah. "I swore not to make any profit," said the man. "How can anyone who is of sound mind make such a vow?" queried the rabbi. Eventually the man admitted that he had actually sworn off gambling profits. Upon hearing this, Rabbi Judah stated: "Blessed are the Sages, who made it a requirement that a man explain the *details* of a vow." (*Vows,* 5, Palestinian Edition. Emphasis added.) Naturally, he did not cancel the man's oath.

In such an intense intellectual atmosphere, there was a good deal of competitiveness. We were, after all, human, and we desired recognition for our accomplishments. Yet we knew that the ideal state was the study of the Talmud for the purpose of glorifying the Almighty, and the holy books, recognizing man's fallibility, contained innumerable admonitions on this matter. The book of *Vows* was no exception, stating at one point that a man ought not to learn so that people should refer to him as "rabbi." Rather, he should study for its own sake and the honor he sought would then come to him anyway. (*Vows,* 62a, Babylonian Edition.)

153

When class ended, nearly two hours later, we all went back to the dining room for lunch. It had been an intellectually stimulating morning for me, and though I was a bit tired, I felt relaxed and happy. I had been able to follow the discussion, more or less, my learning partner seemed ideal, and the rebbe was nothing short of inspiring.

The food, however, was less than inspiring. It was standard institutional fare, but then I had not come to the Gates of Israel Yeshiva to eat! I noticed that a boy seated next to me had a jar of pickles in front of him. "Where did you get those?" I asked. "At the grocery store," he replied. Within a month, I, too, began buying things at the nearby grocery store, with the five dollars a week my father sent me, items such as soda, packages of cake, salami, pickles and my favorite brand of catsup. In an environment where there was not much else to succumb to in the way of earthly desires, such small pleasures assumed great importance, not only enlivening my meals but permitting me, in an odd sort of way, to add a touch of individuality to a way of life that generally demanded strict conformity to a myriad of written and unwritten rules.

After lunch, we returned to the House of Study for the afternoon prayers. Following that we had secular studies. Although state law required that the Yeshiva teach its students certain subjects, it was clear from the attitudes of the Yeshiva administration and those of the older students that subjects such as world history, geometry and physics were insignificant compared to our religious studies. We were taught that all knowledge, religious and secular, was to be found in the Talmud. One needed only to know where to look in order to find it.

True, there were older boys who went to college even though this was not a state requirement, but that fact taken alone would be misleading, for it might lead to the assumption that the Yeshiva approved of college. Nothing could be further from the truth. Students were allowed to go only at night after having spent an entire day in Talmudic study, and only once or twice a week at that. Why, then, did the Yeshiva even permit boys to go? Simply because it realized that a person had to earn a living, too, and that there were not enough positions in religious occupations for everyone.

In fact, it was not the explicit purpose of the Yeshiva to train rabbis. The majority of students who went there did not become rabbis of synagogues or teachers of the Talmud. The idea was that after spending a number of years in the Yeshiva a person would become sufficiently knowledgeable to lead a truly religious existence for the rest of his life. This meant that he would be the sort of person who would always find time to study the Talmud for a few hours a day even if he had a full-time worldly job. Moreover, he would be sure to send his own children to yeshivas.

Nevertheless, the pinnacle of glory in the world of the Yeshiva was to become a member of that select group, limited in size only by necessity, who were to dedicate their entire lives to the study of G-d's wisdom and teachings. And everyone was given to believe that, potentially, he, too, could belong to this elite. Generally speaking, the criteria that were applied were proficiency in learning, determination to excel and devoutness. Obviously, the brighter the person, the greater his chances. At the same time, many who were brilliant did not succeed, usually because of a lack of will or some other human failing, while many who succeeded did so not so much by virtue of intelligence as through sheer effort and diligence.

There was the story of a boy who had excelled in his studies at the Yeshiva, and was considered a fine person as well, the sort who would look for opportunities to help others. Finally, he was extremely careful in his observance of the commandments. The Rosh Yeshiva (Head of the Yeshiva) took a special liking to him, regarding him as a model student.

One day the boy decided to go to law school. This act shocked the Yeshiva, but perhaps no one was more hurt than the Head of the Yeshiva himself. Every time the student would come to the house of the Head of the Yeshiva, the rabbi would say: "Why did you go to law school? Why did you do this?" Over and over again, the same question. The rabbi simply could not accept that such a student could turn his back on the yeshiva world. And no matter how strenuously the young man attempted to explain his decision it was all to no avail, for the result was still the same. He had forsaken the world of his forefathers for the temptations that lay beyond it.

In our yeshiva, obviously, the way to win favor in the eyes of the rabbis was to follow the maxim in the Book of Joshua: "And thou shalt study it [the Torah] day and night" (Joshua 1:8). Total involvement in Talmudic study was the highest achievable goal, and we all looked up to those who had attained or even come close to attaining it.

While many of the Talmud's laws dealt with matters that no longer seemed applicable, such as rites connected with the ancient Temple, this had no effect on our perception of their significance, for we fervently believed in the coming of the Messiah and the return of the Jews to an Israel that would be governed by G-d's laws as they had been given on Mount Sinai. Moreover, we *knew* that each day spent studying and observing G-d's commandments brought the coming of the Messiah one step closer.

Our teachers in the English studies department were, of

course, unaware of all this. They taught, for the most part, in the public schools of the city. For them this was an extra job. Still, they recognized that we did not attach great significance to what we learned in those courses. In truth, even if we had been interested in these subjects, it would have been difficult to concentrate, for by midafternoon we had already expended a tremendous amount of our mental energy on the Talmud.

Nonetheless, in those early days, my past life retained a sufficient hold on my perceptions to keep alive my interest in English, French, Algebra and the like. I had, after all, received a solid secular education at the Light of Abraham Yeshiva back in New York. As time passed, however, it became clear that the brand of Orthodoxy practiced by those in the Light of Abraham Yeshiva was as different from that to which I was now being exposed as it was from the non-Orthodox Jewish community.

The Light of Abraham Yeshiva actually blended the religious with the secular. While there were yeshiva high schools, attended by many of the graduates of my elementary school, that had a similar viewpoint, those who ran the Gates of Israel Yeshiva felt that such a synthesis was impossible. In their opinion, the two could never be on an equal or even nearly equal footing, and to suggest as much insulted and degraded the holiness of the Jews' true purpose in life.

There might be those outside the Orthodox Jewish world who equated keeping the Sabbath, eating kosher food only, wearing a skullcap and carrying out various other laws with being an Orthodox Jew, but those at the Yeshiva, and the thousands who supported this institution and others like it, felt otherwise. They looked down upon Jews who wore small, knitted yarmulkes, calling these head coverings "bottlecaps." They felt that those Jews who went to the beach, movies and nightclubs were people who wanted to have their cake and eat it, too, to partake of worldly pleasures and still be thought Orthodox Jews.

They considered themselves the authentic carriers of the Orthodox way of life as it had been practiced for centuries, and they were determined not to allow it to become diluted by concessions to the larger society unless absolutely necessary. In their view, and this was driven home to me almost daily at first, there could be no compromise with secularism. If a religious person compromised, then he was by definition no longer religious, for true adherence to the faith meant following it in every respect.

By the time classes ended at 6 P.M., I was exhausted. Thus I was grateful for the brief period of free time before supper at 6:30, and decided to explore my surroundings. In addition to the main complex that housed the Beis haMedrash, classrooms, dormitory and dining room, there was only one other structure, a long two-story, red-brick building that was the residence hall for college-age students. In front of it was a parking lot, and off to the right, a small field overgrown with weeds. Behind it, I could see the outlines of a few houses separated from the field by a rather thin stand of trees.

The air was still. Somewhere a bird chirped, its voice punctuating the silence around me. I felt strange, but could not immediately comprehend the reason for it. Then I realized why. I had been indoors for an entire day! With the exception of rainy days, I could not recall the last time I had let such a long period elapse without going outside, even if for only a moment or two. When I had been at the Light of Abraham Yeshiva, I had at least walked to school in the morning and had also spent about an hour a day playing ball in the schoolyard.

158

The sun was beginning to set directly over the tar-covered roof of the residence hall, spreading deep shades of purple, pink and yellow across the sky. I looked at my watch. It was almost 6:30. Time to eat. Reluctantly, I turned and headed slowly back to the complex.

Over supper I learned that in the evening we were supposed to review whatever had been covered in class during the day. How would I find the strength to do that? I wondered. Yet somehow, by the time everyone returned to the House of Study at 8 P.M., I had managed to get up enough energy to approach the review session with at least some degree of interest. True, I would have preferred to be free to read, play ball or just walk around, but I was involved now in what was almost an endurance contest. After all, each of us had the same schedule, and I was determined to make the grade here.

In view of this strong desire, it was perhaps not surprising that, as Zevulun and I became immersed in reviewing Rav Landau's lecture, I forgot how tired I had been only a short while earlier. We took turns reading. Zevulun would say a few lines and translate while I listened and raised questions, recalling, as I did so, the points that had been made in class. Then we would reverse roles and it would be Zevulun's turn to evaluate and criticize.

Sometimes a certain question would have us both stymied. We would sit hunched over the Talmud, looking at the commentaries, whose words appeared in small print on each side of the Gemara text. These commentaries had been written by rabbis such as Rashi and Rabbenu Nissim, who had lived in Europe hundreds of years after the Talmud had been completed. Yet their work had been so seminal, their insights so profound, that their writings appeared right next to the basic text.

In addition, each tractate of the Talmud was followed by

a section of perhaps equal size that also contained numerous commentaries. These writings probed the meaning of the Talmud's words, elaborating on concepts, raising further questions and, in general, clarifying many points whose meaning was obscure. Moreover, there were literally thousands of books in Hebrew that analyzed the Talmud.

Naturally, beginners were not usually required to absorb too much information. When I had first begun studying Talmud in elementary school, it had been enough simply to understand what the Gemara said. Then, little by little, we were exposed to the writings of the commentaries. At first these were explained to us by the rebbe. Eventually, however, we developed the capacity to locate these sources and read them on our own.

It was not easy, by any means, to develop proficiency in this area. These commentators generally compressed what they had to say in a few words, often without elaboration. As a result, one had to concentrate very hard to grasp the points they made.

By the time an hour had elapsed, the little table at which we sat was piled high with books that had been hastily pulled out from the bookshelves in the back of the room. Being only novices at this sort of thing, we frequently were unable to understand what was going on. But we worked at it! Rav Landau was always there, ready to help, as were other classmates and older students. Still, the best solution was to try to do it on one's own.

For me, the Talmud was the most brilliant work in the world, and I loved it for that alone. More important, it was the word of G-d as explained by the holy rabbis. Constant study of the Talmud tended to sharpen the brain, thereby affecting us in many other ways. This ranged from the quality of our casual banter to the relative ease with which we were able to master our secular studies without spending overmuch time on them.

At 9:30 P.M., the learning part of the day finally ended. We put our Gemaras away and placed hats over our skullcaps for the evening service. The reason for wearing a hat was that praying was comparable to making an appearance before a king. Certainly when one prayed before the King of kings, one dressed in a dignified manner, and wearing a hat (preferably black, because black was considered a symbol of modesty) was deemed appropriate.

The evening service was conducted with the same depth of feeling as that held in the morning. And why should it have been different? G-d was always present, and His expectations must surely be higher of those who have given themselves over to serve Him. Again there was the pause before the Shema resounded through the room, and as I said the words that night, they seemed to have acquired added meaning as I put them into the context of the day's activities:

You shall love the Lord your G-d with all your heart, and with all your soul, and with all your might. And these words which I command you today shall be in your heart. You shall teach them diligently to your children and you shall speak of them when you are sitting at home and when you walk by the way.

This combination of prayer and study, rationalism and emotionalism blending harmoniously with one another, each satisfying basic human needs, made the Yeshiva way of life beautiful and edifying to me. Each of the eighteen blessings that we said that night in the Amidah carried its own spiritual message: "Sound the great ram's horn for our freedom." . . . "May all wickedness be lost instantly." . . . "Grant a perfect healing to all our wounds."

The Sages had given numerous reasons why there were eighteen blessings: the three Patriarchs Abraham, Isaac and Jacob were mentioned eighteen times in the Bible; there were eighteen vertebrae in the spinal column; and G-d's name appeared eighteen times in the Shema.

Generally speaking, the prayers took the place of the sacrifices that had been customarily offered in the days of the Temple. Though ideally prayer should be spontaneous and come from the heart, the rabbis recognized that the average person might find it difficult to express himself adequately. Thus specific prayers were composed. Most important, the prayers were designed to keep alive the idea of a Jewish people bound together by the laws of the Torah and by a desire to return someday to the Holy Land. If not for these prayers, said three times every day of their lives, the collective consciousness of the Jews as a people would surely have been greatly weakened and perhaps even obliterated over the centuries.

By the time we had finished praying, it was almost 10 P.M. We were now free until 11:30, when we were expected to go to sleep (a rule often violated, with only occasional repercussions). There was a concession in the basement of the building, and I can still remember standing in line to buy a burnt, flattened frankfurter, some potato chips and a bottle of soda. In a long room next door stood a green, battered Ping-Pong table, lit only by a naked bulb, which, if nothing else, provided a convenient excuse for missing a shot if you looked at it for longer than a second or two. This was our evening recreation.

Before I knew it, it was 11:30. I went upstairs to the room. My roommates were already asleep. Undressing in silence, I glanced out the window. The bluish light of a television set illuminated the window of a house a half-block away. It might as well have been a million miles. The stars in the sky, though infinitely farther away than that television set, were closer to me. I said my nightly prayers, lay down in bed and before long fell fast asleep.

As the days became weeks

and the weeks turned into months, I lost interest in the outside world, even to the point of sometimes cutting English classes to study the Talmud. Though I corresponded with my parents and even went home for two brief intervals during that year, it was no longer the same. My contacts were too short-lived and superficial—two weeks at home out of nine months. Though I said nothing, after a day or two at home I wanted to return to my new-found utopia.

It was as my Israeli roommate, Yehuda, had predicted. I no longer chafed at the rules and regulations of the Yeshiva. Naturally, socializing with girls, listening to the radio and attending movies were forbidden; they were a waste of time, time that was precious, for was not this world merely a preparation for the world to come? The institution's overriding philosophy was that Torah study was the most important purpose in life. Thus anything that did not directly contribute to it was potentially disruptive and unworthy of attention.

Many nights I would stay awake in the House of Study poring over the Talmud. It was difficult, however, to concentrate past midnight, and when that happened I often discussed religion with the older students. While there were boys who never seemed to think about it, I had a burning desire to believe completely in G-d, to *know* that He existed. On many occasions I was plagued by doubt and uncertainty. I found it difficult to accept the idea that by definition faith could not be proven.

I especially recollect standing near the back of the House of Study late one evening, hours after the evening service, conversing animatedly with a youth of about twenty, when I suddenly became totally convinced of G-d's existence. Maybe it was a combination of the lateness of the hour and the strength of my desire to believe in what would give me peace of mind. Possibly it was due to the flickering memorial candles that burned in the back of the room, whose flames cast eerie shadows on the tomes of the Talmud that stood in the bookcases along the wall. I felt a tremendous sense of relief and happiness. Now I could continue my studies without questioning my faith. Alas, a few days later, the old questions and uncertainties returned.

To come so close and still doubt was supremely frustrating and galling. Childishly perhaps, I felt as though my efforts deserved to be rewarded by a sign. I knew that G-d was all around me and His handiwork was evident throughout the length and breadth of the earth, but could G-d not give even one small sign of recognition to me?

Few boys could maintain the intensity of complete involvement in Torah at all times. True, there were some who were fanatics. Compared to them, I was almost heretical. Some of these individuals would not talk about anything except what was in the holy books. They would pray for a half-hour longer than the others, often missing meals and free time, and even coming late, on occasion, to the learning period.

On the other side were those who did not appear really to belong to the Yeshiva at all. They studied little, dressed in more modern clothes than the rest of us and seemed, by their general demeanor, alienated from the institution. More often than not their behavior and occasional antics were tolerated because the Yeshiva wanted to reach them. Still, there was a point beyond which even these boys could not go, and when that line was crossed, they were usually expelled. Often "solid" students were assigned to learn with such youths in the hope that through exhortation or by setting an example they might properly influence them.

The majority of students, however, fell somewhere in the middle, vacillating between intense devoutness and asceticism and concern with more mundane matters. Even those who were extreme in their beliefs tended to mellow as they left adolescence and grew into early manhood, often striking a happy medium that contrasted sharply with their earlier years.

On the whole, however, our lives were concerned with religion; we lived in a world whose entire raison d'être was bounded by faith. Even our infrequent rebellious acts demonstrated how bound up we were with this way of life. Though we might not be paragons of virtue at all times, the way of life of our rabbis, who were learning almost constantly, inspired us and combined with the total environment of the Yeshiva to make true saintliness seem possible and attainable—that is, until the pressures of earning a living forced out all but the best.

Needless to say, the outside world knew little of this. To the residents in the neighborhood, we must have all looked the same, with our black hats, yarmulkes, floppy jackets and the pallor on our faces that came from spending so much time indoors.

Temptation affected nearly everyone, in varying degrees, of course. I had been in the Yeshiva about eight months when suddenly one evening after supper I had an uncontrollable desire to see a movie, something which, incidentally, I had done on an average of about once a month before coming to the Yeshiva. Making up an excuse about not feeling well to my learning partner, I left via a back exit.

As I sneaked out of the building, I had the distinct impression that I was followed. That impression rapidly became a certainty as I glanced over my shoulder and saw one of the older boys whom I knew only on sight walking behind me. I ducked quickly into an alley that ran between two side streets, but it was no use. He was still behind me three blocks later. After much dodging and twisting, I finally managed to lose him and reached the theater undetected. I had not even looked to see what film was being shown, but it would have made no difference. I simply wanted to get out. As it turned out, *Ben-Hur* was playing. Though it had already won acclaim from the movie critics, I had no idea, for I had not read a newspaper in months. To me, it was an action-packed adventure film, and I thoroughly enjoyed it.

While most of us disliked individuals who made it their business to report and spy on others, we also tended to view them as a necessary evil. The Yeshiva, for its part, knew that students committed infractions but chose to ignore them so long as they happened only occasionally. In at least a few cases, those who followed us around were simply zealous guardians of the faith and their activities did not have a formal stamp of approval from the Yeshiva.

The institution recognized, however reluctantly, that adolescents needed some form of recreation besides Ping-Pong in a basement room. As a result, Friday afternoons were set aside for playing ball. One could not, of course, allow an entire day to be wasted and so we studied Talmud until 12:30, but after that we were free until the setting sun ushered in the Sabbath.

Yehuda and I would generally go to the local Jewish community center, where we could swim, play basketball and really stretch our legs for the first time in a week. This was also one of the few opportunities we had for contact with nonmembers of the Yeshiva community. For the most part, such contact was fleeting and superficial. I might play a basketball game or two with some other boys, but, if nothing else, the yarmulke and woolen fringes that I wore while chasing after the ball set me apart from the rest of the group.

The Yeshiva boys did not mingle with the others except at times like this. We simply had little in common with them. For example, many of the Yeshiva boys would, after leaving the center, go to the mikvah (ritual bath) to immerse and purify themselves for the Sabbath, while most of those who were not from the Yeshiva would go upstairs to the cafeteria and play the jukebox.

Some of the rebbes at the Yeshiva looked with disfavor upon our going to the center, preferring that we confine our ball-playing to the field behind the Yeshiva. Others took a more tolerant view. Rav Morris, who had arrived at the Yeshiva seventeen years earlier wearing, of all things, a pair of jeans, came from a nonobservant home and had barely known Hebrew at the time, much less the Talmud. He was, however, blessed with a wonderful mind. Through enormous effort he succeeded, within a short period, in becoming one of the top students in the Yeshiva. When still in his twenties, he was chosen to be a rebbe in the high school division.

Rav Morris was a sincere and dedicated man; but he

struck many of us as being somewhat inflexible. Even by our standards, he seemed to attach undue importance to the ritual aspects of religion. He would become visibly annoyed, his face fixed in a scowl, if a boy came to the morning service three or four minutes late. His appearance was as clear an indication of the man's personality as anything else. A light-complexioned man who rarely smiled, his dress was immaculate and his beard always neatly trimmed. His clear blue, deep-set eyes bored right through you, looking, it seemed to me, for weaknesses.

At services he looked directly ahead, neither moving nor swaying, a ramrod-straight figure, parts of a navy-blue pin-striped suit visible beneath his prayer shawl. Every once in a while he would raise his arms skyward, but even this was done in a restrained manner, with the outstretched tips of the fingers of both hands held together at the exact same height. Yet none could question or doubt Rabbi Morris' devotion to his students. He was always available, ready to answer a student's query or review a portion of the Talmud with him. Whatever he demanded from others he demanded of himself as well. In all the time I spent at the Yeshiva, I never saw him come late for services, classes, or any other gathering.

My rebbe, Rav Landau, was completely different. He, too, was dedicated to the Talmud and to his students, but he was a far more easygoing man. He recognized that the shortcomings displayed by some of us were human failings, to be expected in adolescents who were only beginning to approach maturity. His dress was not immaculate, but that mattered little to Rav Landau. All that mattered to him was involvement in learning.

As I look back, the clearest image I have of Rav Landau is one of intense absorption: He is standing by the wooden, unpainted shtender in the Beis haMedrash, staring out into space, twirling the tiny curls in his black beard. I have just asked him a question, and he has a beautiful peaceful expression on his face as he mulls over the myriad of possibilities it has raised. It is not that my point is so deep—it is simply that Rav Landau's knowledge is so encyclopedic and his mind so original that he recognizes an almost infinite number of implications in any issue that is raised.

He would always be eight steps ahead of the class, and as he proceeded to work out a problem his countenance would become enraptured. The joy that lit up his face was an inspiration to me. I, too, wanted to reach that level. He was always encouraging us to think deeply. Unlike Rav Morris, he was not so concerned that one know every detail of a Talmudic discussion. Rather, his goal was to get us to appreciate the full range and scope of a discussion, to catch a glimpse and be part of the rarefied atmosphere that surely must have prevailed in the Babylonian and Palestinian academies of old. To Rav Landau, Talmudic study was sheer ecstasy, and his interpretations of it were so delicately constructed as to be almost poetic.

Because he was so involved in the Talmud, Rav Landau tended to neglect many everyday matters. He was fortunate to have married a woman who was a practical person with both feet firmly planted on the ground. Rav Landau was so "fahrteefed" (totally absorbed) in his own world that he frequently could be seen returning at odd hours to the Yeshiva to pick up something he had forgotten. Often I saw him walking in zigzag fashion along the street, totally oblivious to everything but what was on his mind.

There were other rebbes, with whom I had less familiarity. I was taking a walk one evening when I heard footsteps behind me. Turning, I recognized Rav Sperling. A dour-faced, hollow-cheeked man, he was the rebbe of the class below me and had been, for a short time, the administrator of the high school, during which he had acquired a reputation as a strict disciplinarian. Falling into step with me, Rav Sperling asked how I was coming along. "Fine," I said. We continued talking. It was around the time of the High Holy Days and repentance was very much on everyone's mind. The conversation turned to that subject.

Suddenly, without thinking, I blurted out: "Rav Sperling, what happens to a person who sins and does not repent?" Rav Sperling seemed momentarily taken aback. It was one thing to raise such a matter in the context of a Talmudic discussion, but in a personal conversation my question was a rather forward one. However, he quickly recovered his composure. By this time we had reached his house. He stopped beneath a large spreading oak tree and, looking me directly in the eye, said, "You know what happens? I'll tell you what: You burn in Hell. And do you know how hot it is?" I was too frightened to reply, but he waited expectantly. "No," I said in a small voice. "Light a match; it's sixty times as hot!" I was terrified, and as I told him good night, I could feel my heart rapidly going thump, thump, thump. "I don't mean to scare you, Naftoli," he said, "but this is a serious matter. I hope you will think about it."

Judaism preached adherence to G-d's laws out of love, not fear, but many individuals could follow the laws only if they feared the consequences. In point of fact, such an approach was the exception at the Yeshiva, not the rule. No other rebbe ever suggested such an idea to me, and even Rav Sperling never said anything of the sort to me again.

The older rebbes who taught in the senior division were more distant. Yet I respected and revered them unquestioningly. Their lives were a main topic of conversation among the boys. There was Reb Eliezer (for some reason, he was referred to only by his first name). An older man, he had fled the Nazis in World War II and had escaped, but the rest of his family had not been so fortunate. He had, therefore, completely thrown himself into learning the Talmud at the time, saying, "I must study Torah while my parents are being killed, for if not I will surely lose my sanity."

This saintly man's interest in the boys in the Yeshiva was unparalleled. Though he had children of his own, he regarded all the students in the Yeshiva as his sons. He served as the Mashgiach, or Dean, of the school. As such he offered us moral and ethical guidance. If someone had a personal problem that his own rebbe was unable to solve or that the boy did not want to disclose to the rebbe, Reb Eliezer was the man to whom one could go.

Moreover, every Sabbath afternoon he would give what was known as a mussar shmooz. This was a talk, lasting about an hour and a half, that took place shortly before the Sabbath ended. Essentially, its purpose was to exhort us to improve our moral behavior, to be more considerate toward others, to resist worldly temptation and to pray with greater sincerity. It was true that learning was the foundation stone of the Yeshiva, but without ethical and righteous conduct intellectual achievements were meaningless, and it was Reb Eliezer's duty to constantly remind us of this.

He did not simply quote to us from the Sages. No, he personalized everything. He was intimately familiar with all that went on inside the Yeshiva, and he used his talks as a forum for expressing his views about life there in general and our conduct in particular.

Of short stature, he would sit in his chair in the classroom looking out at us, his favorites clustered in a semicircle around him, with the rest of us seated behind in chairs or on the window sills, and the late-comers standing in the back. As the twilight gave way to darkness in the small room, Reb Eliezer's tiny figure became a silhouette outlined against the wall, recognizable only by the gray beard that bobbed up and down as he gesticulated to emphasize his arguments. He knew just when to pause and when to speak, when to raise his voice and when to lower it. We all listened intently, for in his words lay not only wisdom, not only the key to understanding the philosophy of the Yeshiva, but also irony, wit and empathy with the hard road we had chosen.

One of his most famous talks concerned a time when some of the boys, being hungry, had sneaked into the kitchen late one night, and stolen some bananas from the refrigerator. Hearing nothing about it for a few days afterward, they assumed that their crime had gone undetected. Thus they were perhaps more surprised than anyone else when, suddenly, in the midst of a lecture about the true way to act, Reb Eliezer began talking mockingly about bananas.

"I heard," he said in Yiddish (he always spoke in his native tongue), "that there are bochorim [boys] here who like bananas. That's what they like. Three, four, five, ten, twenty bananas! That's what they eat—like monkeys!" Everyone shifted uncomfortably in his chair. "Who makes a meal out of bananas? Monkeys, not human beings! It's a real question. Can you teach Torah to monkeys? I'll have to think about it." Over and over again until everyone began laughing, soft chuckles at first, then changing to open laughter as it became evident that Reb Eliezer was exaggerating. Nevertheless, the point was made. It was not the proper thing to do, and it never happened again.

Reb Eliezer managed to weave into his discourses such topics as sports, college and world politics. For us, encased

172

in our cocoon, such discussions were fascinating, and we hung on every word, eagerly absorbing whatever was said. To us it was incredible that he knew so much about secular subjects.

Nothing could prevent Reb Eliezer from coming to the Yeshiva. In the worst snowstorm, he came from blocks away, the raw wind whipping at his face, the snow swirling around his small frame, barely five feet tall, carrying his copy of the Talmud beneath his arm against his dark-blue coat. How this man was able to find time to learn about baseball, I will never know, yet he managed. He once talked for an hour about the game, ridiculing the purpose of the sport, until by the time he was through I wondered why I ever played it.

We were encouraged in this way and in others to play down the physical aspects of our lives and to give precedence to that which was spiritual. The Torah was G-d's priceless gift to His people. How dare we throw it away?

Still, there was one "physical" area that was often a topic of conversation. I don't know how many times I heard the story (you never knew how it got started or how true it was) about the Yeshiva boy who beat up ten Jew-haters single-handedly as they taunted him on his way to the local grocery store, or wherever he was walking. Every yeshiva had such mythical heroes who became part of the institution's informal social history. Deep down most of us knew the tale was exaggerated at best, untrue at worst; yet our desire to indulge in our fantasies prevented us from asking too many details. Most of us were not fighters. Our culture did not reward or even encourage such behavior. And although we may have dreamed about how we would gain revenge on the neighborhood bullies, our visions were, on the whole, more spiritual.

Finally, there was the Rosh or Head of the Yeshiva. As befitted his position, he was regarded as the most erudite scholar in the institution and was one of the most respected rabbis in the world. It was said of him that he knew all sixty-three volumes of the Talmud by the time he was sixteen. This was a prodigious achievement, since even among those who spent their entire lives studying only a handful knew the entire Talmud from beginning to end.

The Rosh Yeshiva had been raised in Eastern Europe and had come to America before World War II. He had founded and guided the Yeshiva, and its fine reputation was greatly enhanced by his dynamic leadership. His appearance was majestic, his bearing proud. Of medium height, with a long, flowing gray beard, he always wore a large broad-brimmed black hat, with a matching double-breasted long coat. During my stay in the Yeshiva, I had no contact with him whatsoever, but then who was I? One among hundreds, a beginner. I knew, however, that someday, if I lasted, I would be in his class, which was the highest in the school.

He lectured only once a week or so, but his class was so profound that it took an entire week for the students, knowledgeable as they were, to prepare for it. Though I never spoke with him, I always felt his presence in an intimate manner, for he symbolized the Yeshiva, both inside its walls and to the world at large. At least a tiny bit of his greatness rubbed off on me, if only through people knowing I attended an institution headed by him.

Each class in the Yeshiva was comprised of students whose level of understanding was roughly equal. They ranged from the beginners' group, made up of those who were learning Gemara for the first time, to those in the highest class, who could study on their own. Though we might gain more from a learned and knowledgeable partner, the rebbes encouraged us to work with boys who were just beginning. In addition to the satisfaction that came from giving of oneself, teaching others forced me to work out the arguments carefully, to be prepared to both explain and defend them. In fact, not until I began working with another boy in my spare time, one who had never studied Talmud, did I truly begin to appreciate the exquisite beauty inherent in the logical arguments presented by the Sages.

I had once asked Rav Landau why it was necessary to know all the arguments as they developed in the course of a Talmudic debate. Why not, I wondered, simply learn the conclusion and not bother with the stages of reasoning that led up to it? Rav Landau's explanation was that the progression of arguments showed one all the different aspects of the law and that only when one saw all the difficulties surrounding the law could one fully grasp the clarity and wisdom of the decisions. Perhaps the best way to illustrate the value of our method of learning would be to paraphrase a portion of the Talmud that I had once learned and which I taught to a younger, less advanced student at the Yeshiva:

"If a person asked his neighbor or friend to watch over his animal or utensil and it was then stolen or lost, who should be compensated if the thief was caught? (The fine, assuming the object was recovered intact, was double its value.) If, when the theft was discovered, the guardian immediately paid the owner the value of the lost object, then the thief should pay the fine to the guardian as a reward for his willingness to compensate the owner. If, on the other hand, the guardian, declining to make up the loss to the owner, swore instead that he had not stolen the object (he had this option as well), then if the thief was caught, the 'double fine' should, of course, go to the owner of the animal or utensil.

"What would happen," asked the Talmud, "if, when the

thief was apprehended, it was discovered that he had already sold or slaughtered the animal? He would then be required to pay four times its value in the case of a sheep and five times its worth if it were a bull." This immediately raised the question "Why four times in one instance and five in the other?" "Because," was the answer, "a sheep might become tired, making it necessary for the thief to carry it over his shoulders while on his way to the marketplace to sell it. As a result, the Torah took pity on the thief, lowering the fine somewhat. In the case of a bull, however, all the thief had to do was lead it to town." The fact that the Torah showed compassion toward the thief was but one example of Judaism's concern with the well-being of all people, no matter what their station in life.

The discussion would go back and forth, increasing in complexity, with all sorts of new issues being raised. A discussion would ensue as to whether one could buy something which had not yet come into existence. Rav Meir would be cited as having said that in the case of a palm tree this was true since it was sure to grow except in the event of a flood. This would then be applied to the wool which grew on a sheep and the offspring of a cow. To an outsider it may all have seemed pointless, but to us these discussions were the staff of life, as important today as they had been when first set down by the Sages of old.

What was required of us as yeshiva students was clearly far more than was expected of most adolescents. To spend long hours bent over ancient books, concentrating on every word, ever conscious of the need to reach higher and higher levels of understanding and spirituality, was most demanding. Thus the holiday of Purim was a welcome occasion. A twenty-four-hour affair that lasted from sunset to sunset, it commemorated the triumph of the Jews, in about 450 B.C.E. over their Persian persecutor Haman, who was King Ahasuerus' vizier. The name "Purim" was taken from the word "pur," or "lottery," the method by which Haman selected the date on which he would have all the Jews, men, women and children, killed. Through the intervention of the Jewish queen, Esther, and her uncle, Mordecai, the Jews were saved, winning a great victory over Haman and his allies. On Purim Eve the story was read from the Scroll of Esther, referred to as the Megillah.

As holidays went in the Jewish religion, Purim was easy to observe. It lasted one day and had far fewer obligations than, say, Passover or Succoth. Yet at the Yeshiva it was celebrated as a major event. This was because over time it had become the one day a year when, as approved by law, everyone could truly let himself go. There was a rabbinic injunction that on Purim one should drink until he could no longer tell the difference between "Cursed be Haman" and "Blessed be Mordecai." During the rest of the year nobody drank except after making the holy benediction over wine on Sabbath and holidays.

Bottles of whiskey, wine and beer would appear as if by magic, and we would happily consume perhaps five times as much as we drank during the entire remainder of the year. I can remember more than one fellow, including myself, whose desire for liquor was permanently quenched by our excesses on that day. In the evening, after the service, we would dance with reckless abandon through the long halls of the Yeshiva, singing the Lord's praises, thanking him for having delivered us:

> For out of Zion shall come forth Torah
> and the word of the Lord from Jerusalem.

Later on in the evening, everyone would go to his rebbe's house to be with him on this happy night, to eat a little, sing a little, dance a little, and above all to hear some "Purim Torah." This was generally a satirical presentation that made light of what we took so seriously during the year. For example, Rav Landau would take a word in the daily prayers, add up its numerical value, multiply it by, say, five, subtract from it the numerical value of another randomly chosen word, and presto! we would now know why there were 287 students in the Yeshiva.

The boys would join in as well, giving their own novel interpretations. A boy might point out that the Hebrew letters for "rebbe" equaled 212—which, in degrees Fahrenheit, is the boiling point of water. Naturally, Hebrew was a holy language and we were not really ridiculing it in a serious way. These games were simply an expression of release and enjoyment. Explanations of the sort given above were unheard of on any other day of the year.

The high point of the holiday was the Purim play put on by the boys in the Yeshiva, which lampooned life in the institution. Nothing was sacred. Students who had told on others became the butt of jokes, the indigestibility of the food was noted, and the crowded facilities parodied. Even the rebbes themselves were roasted. Boys would dress up, play the role of the various rebbes and present skits and songs about them.

In reality, these antics provided the faculty with a rare opportunity to see just how the boys perceived them, for during the year such attitudes never surfaced. In sum, though, it was one day out of three hundred and sixty-five, and the way in which we behaved served in itself to emphasize the austerity and seriousness of purpose that characterized our daily life in the Yeshiva.

The holiday of Shevuoth (Pentecost) was an excellent example of our concern with reaching a certain level of holiness. Shevuoth celebrated the giving of the Torah on Mount Sinai. Coming seven weeks after Passover, which commemorated our liberation from Egypt, it was a joyous occasion, for it was only when the Torah was given that the Jews truly became a cohesive force, unified through their acceptance of the yoke of the Lord's Kingdom.

In the Yeshiva the holiday assumed special significance because of the custom associated with it of staying awake the whole night and studying the Talmud. This was done in Orthodox communities throughout the world, but in the Yeshiva it was observed in the fullest sense. Elsewhere the average person might become tired about three or four in the morning and spend the rest of the time engaged in conversation. This rarely happened to us, for we had been conditioned for such an effort by all the hours spent studying during the year. No matter what time one walked into the Beis haMedrash on that night, one could see well over a hundred boys swaying back and forth as they looked at the folio pages.

Every once in a while one could make out a voice distinct from the many: "Rebbe Yehuda says" or "So what's the question?" and then answering himself in a lilting, singsong tone: "The question is . . ." Others would be pacing the length and width of the House of Study deeply engrossed in thought, pausing every now and then before continuing. Dovid Halberstam would be looking out the window, but you knew what he was thinking about. An older man, he had left a well-paying job in industry to learn here day and night. Yaakov Shulman, one of the best students in the Rosh Yeshiva's class, would be leaning backward in his chair, lost

179

in thought. Every now and then, the chair would come forward, its legs hitting the floor with a bang, as Yaakov, seized with inspiration, jumped up and ran to the back of the room to search for this or that commentary.

In truth, this scene was typical of the entire year. The Beis haMedrash was never empty, but the night of Shevuoth was something special. As a child my father, to encourage me to stay up and learn, had told me that for those who learn on that night there existed the possibility that if they looked at the sky at exactly midnight, the blackness of the heavens would part for a split second and beyond them Paradise itself would be revealed, and if at that moment one made a wish, it would be fulfilled. Of course, my father reminded me, one had to study hard and look up at exactly the right time. A second too late and one would simply have to wait patiently until the following year.

In the Yeshiva, such a story was hardly necessary. We knew the reason for staying up quite clearly. It was the night of the giving of the Law, and for such an occasion one had to be pure in body and in soul, just as the ancient Israelites had been when G-d revealed Himself on Mount Sinai and gave us the Ten Commandments. To make things more realistic, we had gone out during the day and gathered greens in the field by the Yeshiva, for Mount Sinai, despite its desert location, had been a green mountain in those days. Unlike on Passover, there were no special foods to partake of except for a dairy meal, eaten, according to some rabbis, to acknowledge that Palestine was a land flowing with *milk* and honey. Nor did we sit in special huts, as we did on Succoth. Yet Shevuoth was supremely important because it celebrated the most momentous event in our history.

So ended my first year at the Gates of Israel Yeshiva. A week after Shevuoth I went home and began preparing for the summer vacation at Camp Tikvath Shalom.

There were still close to three weeks before I left for camp, and I spent much of that time getting together with my old neighborhood friends from the Light of Abraham Yeshiva.

When I first saw them, there was a feeling of distance between us. In the life of a fourteen- or fifteen-year-old a year is a long time. My friends had stayed in New York and were, for the most part, attending school together. From talking with them, I discovered just how different their experience had been from my own. They were primarily interested in sports, especially basketball, and when they compared the other yeshiva high school teams their institutions had competed with, I felt very left out.

This was equally true of their discussions about professional sports. I had always been a Brooklyn Dodger fan, even though I lived in Manhattan. I would enthusiastically defend their merits to my friends, most of whom were Giant or Yankee fans. Our loyalties to these teams continued even after 1957, when the Giants and Dodgers moved to California. But now I had nothing to say. At Gates of Israel, I had completely lost track of such things and found the conversation totally irrelevant at first. They, in turn, looked at me as if I were a creature from outer space, especially after I made some fumbling attempts at describing my current life style. They simply could not comprehend why anyone would want to live like that—no movies, dances, ice skating or similar recreations. Unable to express myself adequately about the beauty of yeshiva life, I found that I, too, was beginning to have some doubts.

There was only one boy living in my neighborhood who had gone to the Yeshiva with me, and I did not particularly care for him. My father's encouragement, pride and happiness that I was becoming a "talmid chachem" were not enough to offset my feelings of estrangement. I was lonely, and eagerly looked forward to the day when I would leave for Camp Tikvath Shalom.

Yet even camp proved disappointing. Daniel, the counselor who had so influenced me the previous summer, had not returned. Besides, we had not been close in the Yeshiva. It was as if he felt his duty was done. He had brought me there and the rest was up to me. I was a junior counselor and therefore more on my own. The counselor I worked with was going to business school by day and a yeshiva at night, certainly not my idea of what a true Ben Torah ("son of learning") should do. Camp life itself was not really geared for study of Torah. Oh, to be sure, compared to other camps, the hour or two a day spent studying was quite a bit, but compared to the Yeshiva it was literally child's play.

Most disturbing, though, was the fact that even the boys in camp now proved difficult to relate to. While they were far more Orthodox than my friends from the city, they were not nearly as involved in religion as I and my friends at Gates of Israel had been. They attended schools in New York for the most part, lived at home, watched television, and cared almost as much about secular subjects as their religious ones. One of them, a boy named Aryeh Sheingold, had brought a chemistry set to play with during his spare time, and as I talked with him, I began to realize how little I knew. My course in science at the Yeshiva had not been particularly extensive. Why should we have learned more than the minimum when our immersion in Yeshiva life emphasized the supreme importance of religion? The conviction that I had not learned much in nonreligious subjects was further strengthened by subsequent conversations with other boys. The previous year we had all been more or less equal in terms of general knowledge. But now, a year later, things had changed. No one's world had stopped—it was simply that I had gone in a somewhat different direction and I now lacked the supportive and protective environment of the Yeshiva.

When I returned to Gates of Israel in the fall, there was a gnawing feeling of dissatisfaction deep inside me, a certain unease brought about, I knew, from my contacts with others during the summer. Several times I had been on the verge of mentioning it to my father, but he had seemed so happy at my ability to handle Talmud and at the degree to which I observed the various laws that I simply could not bring myself to speak openly with him about it. Besides, I thought, these problems would surely disappear as I got back into the swing of things. The High Holy Days were coming, and I soon became so absorbed in the preparations for them that the malaise which had gripped me faded quickly into the background. By the time Rosh Hashonah arrived, I was so wrapped up in the purpose and meaning of the holiday that I could think of nothing else.

And the Lord spoke unto Moses saying: Speak unto the children of Israel saying: In the seventh month, on the first day of the month, there shall be for you a solemn day of rest, a memorial announced by the blast of horns, a holy assembly.

Leviticus 24:23–24

This was the passage in the Bible instructing us to observe Rosh Hashonah, the Jewish New Year. This holiday signaled the beginning of a ten-day period during which every Jew is obligated to undergo a period of soul-searching, intense reflection and, above all, repentance. The final day was Yom Kippur, the Day of Atonement.

For us in the Yeshiva, it was a most crucial time. We knew that the hour of judgment was drawing near and we wanted therefore to be extra careful not to commit any offenses in this period. Our souls had already been stirred by the sounding of the shofar, or ram's horn, which took place every day of the month preceding Rosh Hashonah, following the morning service. While throughout the Jewish community it was customary to send greeting cards that read, "May you be inscribed and sealed for a good year," it was our practice (and that of many Orthodox Jews) to express this wish whenever we wrote a letter to a friend or to any fellow Jew during the entire month preceding Rosh Hashonah.

Moreover, we would carefully inspect our tefillin and mezuzahs to ensure that they were still kosher. Nothing could be left to chance. No one wanted to enter the "Days of Awe," as they were known, in anything but a state of complete purity, and this necessitated extra caution in all our behavior. Most significantly perhaps, we were required to approach people we knew and thought we might have offended to beg their forgiveness. This was because prayer on the Day of Atonement atoned for sins that one person had committed against another only if forgiveness had been asked from and granted by the wronged party.

I must have asked that question a hundred times in the days before Rosh Hashonah (although Yom Kippur was actually the deadline, one was not supposed to wait until the last minute). I walked up to each person and said, "Do you forgive me? Do you forgive me?" One never knew who harbored a grudge because of a slight or careless remark.

True, there were times when someone brought up a matter of this sort to the offending party, but for the most part such forgiveness was automatic. At this particular time of year, no one was in the mood to harbor feelings of resentment toward others.

On the day before Rosh Hashonah immediately after having a haircut, everyone in the Yeshiva went to the ritual bath. What this involved was stripping completely naked and allowing one's body to be completely covered by the water.

Upon returning from the baths, I put on my finest attire. It was customary to honor the holiday by wearing at least one new article of clothing. My father had bought me a gray pinstriped suit, and as I took it out of the closet, I suddenly felt homesick. Thinking about his gift reminded me of the times I had accompanied him to the synagogue on the High Holy Days.

The synagogue looked completely different when we arrived that evening for the service. The blue velvet cover that adorned the Holy Ark had been removed. In its place was a white one with gold trimming. Inside the Ark, the Torahs were covered with matching white velvet.

The air was still. The cantor, one of the rebbes in the Yeshiva, began the service: "Bless ye the Lord, who is blessed." "Blessed be the Lord, who is blessed forever and evermore," we responded. A different melody, special for the occasion, was used, and as the congregation joined in, one could feel a certain joy surge through the room. The time was here. G-d was listening to us, paying special attention as He gave us our chance to pour out our hearts and obtain His forgiveness. When we said the silent prayer, we made certain to include the phrase "Remember us unto life, O King who takes delight in life, and inscribe us in the Book

185

of Life, for Thine own sake, O living G-d."

After the service it was the custom for everyone to wish one another a good year before going into the dining room to eat raisin challah and other delicacies that had been prepared for us. As I dipped the challah into a bowl of honey, I said the blessing, "May it be Thy will, O Lord, to renew for us a good and sweet year." Everyone had brought in holy books to read at the table, for we knew the Day of Judgment was imminent and we wanted to make the best possible impression on our Maker at this most important time. The meal was sumptuous: plenty of fish and meat, and all sorts of candies and desserts. It was, however, considered improper to eat almonds, cashews and peanuts, because they tended to increase one's saliva and interfere with one's ability to say the many prayers that would be required of us on the following day.

Though the service began early, at 7 A.M., no one was late. The synagogue was packed with students, rabbis and local residents. Hardly anyone had gone home, for it was deemed a matter of the highest priority that one attend High Holy Day services in a synagogue that emphasized spirituality. We felt that many other synagogues, even though they conducted the services in a strictly Orthodox fashion, tended to suffer because their congregants sometimes treated the holiday as an opportunity not only to pray but to socialize with friends. This was viewed by us as most unbecoming and not the sort of atmosphere in which we wanted to worship.

Not a sound could be heard as Rav Wachtel, one of the most respected rebbes in the Yeshiva, made his way through the crowd. He had a beautiful voice, but that was not the reason for his selection as the cantor for the Mussaf service. It was because he met other, far more important criteria. According to the Code of Jewish Law it was essential that he who led the congregation in prayer be a respected man, learned in Jewish law and a doer of good deeds. He must be over thirty, married and have children so that he could truly speak from the depth of his heart.

The decision on whether a person possessed all these qualities was arrived at by consensus of the congregation. Such consensus was so important that if a candidate saw that his nomination caused dissension, he was required to withdraw, even if it meant, in his view, that an unworthy candidate would be selected in his place. Naturally, there were no such problems with Rav Wachtel, nor with any of the other rebbes who conducted the various portions of the service.

As Rav Wachtel began intoning the words in his deep bass voice, I felt a shiver run up and down my spine. Each word was uttered ever so carefully, the syllables enunciated with great precision. It was the cantor's meditation that introduced the service, an eloquent plea to the Almighty:

Poor in deeds of merit, I am terrified in the presence of Thou who sits on the throne and receives praise from Israel.

I have come to stand and beg before Thee on behalf of Thy nation Israel, who have sent me, though I am neither worthy nor qualified for the task.

And so I beg of Thee, the G-d of Abraham, Isaac and Jacob. O G-d, G-d, O Lord, who is the merciful and gracious G-d of Israel, the Almighty and Revered one, ensure the success of the path in which I walk—to stand and beg mercy on my behalf and for those who have sent me.

Let *them* not be blamed for my sins, do not hold *them* responsible for my wicked deeds, for I am a sinner and a transgressor indeed. [Emphasis added.]

187

Rav Wachtel a sinner? A transgressor? Not worthy nor qualified for this task? As I listened to him say these words with utmost humility and feeling, as I heard him prostrate himself before the Almighty, I began to feel very small. At the start of the service, I had felt as though our community was an elite of sorts. After all, we kept so many commandments, studied day and night. Yet, as I thought of the words being said, I began to have serious doubts about the accuracy of that assumption.

Who was I, anyway? A novice, young in years and in understanding. Here was Rav Wachtel, one of the greatest Torah leaders of our generation, saying publicly that he was poor in worthy deeds. And if that was so, then where did it leave me? I found myself thinking of a thousand trivial things that had concerned me over the past year: taking pride in a new sport jacket, eating delicious french fries at the only kosher delicatessen in town, playing handball with reckless abandon against the dormitory building. And what about the times I had spoken evil of others, addressed others impolitely, thought unclean thoughts? Even as a child I had always been more religiously inclined than many of my friends. A holiday like this, coupled with my present environment, served only to awaken my doubts, fears and need to believe, and, of course, to be forgiven.

In reality, now was not the time for confession of one's sins. That was supposed to be done on Yom Kippur, for Rosh Hashonah was a festival. Nevertheless, it ushered in those terrible days of repentance, terrible because so much hung in the balance. In the time between Rosh Hashonah and Yom Kippur all our deeds of the past year that had been written in The Book would be scrutinized in every detail before being signed and sealed, forever and ever, on the Day of Atonement. This period was our last opportunity to affect the decree, to change our destiny, to lift our eyes heavenward and obtain our merciful G-d's forgiveness.

The reader completed his prayers as we prepared to say the silent Amidah. We stood, feet together, for perhaps thirty or forty minutes, praying and meditating, whispering the words. Then, when everyone had finished, Rav Wachtel began repeating the Amidah aloud, with the congregants answering "Amen" and joining in at the appropriate points in the service.

Finally, we came to one of the most important prayers in the entire liturgy, which opened with the words "Let us tell how holy this day is." The prayer, said on both Rosh Hashonah and Yom Kippur, was first published by Rav Meshullam, son of Kalonymous, who lived in Mainz, Germany, in about the tenth century.

Legend had it that in Mainz there lived a Rav Amnon, who was greatly admired by the Prince of Mainz. The Prince sent for Rav Amnon and offered to give him a ministerial post on one condition—that he change his faith. Rav Amnon replied, "Give me three days to reflect on your request." "All right," said the Prince, "but be certain that you do not take any longer."

Immediately after leaving the Prince's residence, Rav Amnon was seized with remorse. How could he have doubted his faith for even a moment? Why, oh why, had he not said no immediately? Three days passed. The Prince sent three separate messages to Rav Amnon, who had not appeared. Finally, the Prince had Rav Amnon brought before him by force.

"Where is the answer you promised me?" demanded the Prince. "I do not wish to answer you," said Rav Amnon, "and because I spoke without thinking and asked you for three days' time to reflect, which was an expression of un-

189

certainty in my faith, I would now like to pass judgment on myself—namely, that my blasphemous tongue be cut out." The Prince refused, saying, "That would be too light a punishment. Rather, your feet which came not to me when I sent for you should be removed, as well as your other limbs."

This horrible order was carried out and Rav Amnon was brought back to his home, where he lay dying before his wife and children.

Looking at their terror-stricken faces, he said, "This is my just reward for having questioned my faith. I only hope that through my pain and suffering I can atone for my sins and be deserving of a place in the world to come."

This occurred immediately prior to Rosh Hashonah, and when that day came, Rav Amnon summoned forth whatever strength he still possessed and asked that he be carried into the synagogue and placed next to the cantor, "for I wish to glorify the Lord's name before I die." And this is a portion from that stirring prayer, which were the last words uttered by the saintly rabbi:

All mankind passes before Thee like a flock of sheep. . . .

On Rosh Hashonah their destiny is inscribed and on Yom Kippur it is sealed. How many shall depart from this world and how many shall enter it? Who shall live and who shall die? . . . Who shall die by fire and who by water? who by the sword and who by wild beast? who by hunger and who by thirst? . . .

Three days afterward Rav Amnon appeared before his rebbe, Rav Meshullam, and asked that he send this prayer to Jewish communities throughout the world to be read on Rosh Hashonah and Yom Kippur.

Virtually all the ways in which man could perish were enumerated in this devotion, but its essence lay in the martyrdom of Rav Amnon. Despite his horrible sufferings, he was not bitter, and therein lay our lesson. No matter how much travail we had endured, we were not permitted to despair. We needed to trust in G-d, and in so doing transcend the barbarity that existed on this earth. The prayer ended on a hopeful note: "And repentance, prayer, and charity cancel the stern decree."

A week later, Yom Kippur, the Day of Atonement, arrived. The excitement in the Yeshiva was at fever pitch as everyone made his way to the synagogue to hear the Kol Nidre (All Vows) prayer that marked the beginning of a twenty-four-hour period of fasting and prayer. Even Jews who observe no laws honor this day, if they have even a tiny bit of identification with the faith of their fathers. They may only attend synagogue for an hour or two, they may not even pray, but whatever the case, as if driven by some primordial instinct, they come.

We had been preparing for this day all year and especially since the beginning of Rosh Hashonah. The words of the Bible were explicit: "Ye shall do no work at all. It is a statute forever, for all generations to come, in all your dwellings. It shall be for you a sabbath of sabbaths and ye shall afflict your souls in the ninth day of the month, in the evening; from evening to evening shall ye keep your sabbath." (Leviticus 23:31–32.)

It was a beautiful sight. All around me were males dressed in white, their heads covered with white skullcaps. Along the walls of the Beis haMedrash candles and little electric lights glowed in blessed memory of the departed from our community. The gates of heaven had opened and we were now about to make one last, supreme effort to scale the heights and plead our cause.

191

The cantor was Reb Eliezer himself, our esteemed rebbe. It was fitting that the one who concerned himself most with our daily conduct throughout the year should represent us now. If anyone could "cancel the decree," it was Reb Eliezer. In a clear yet trembling voice he began intoning the words:

> By the authority of the heavenly court,
> By the authority of the earthly court,
> With the consent of the Lord,
> And with the knowledge of the congregation,
> We now declare it permissible to pray with transgressors.

The Torahs had been taken out for the occasion, with the most respected rebbes in the Yeshiva being given the honor of holding them. Their rods jutted out from the tops, covered with tinkling silver crowns. Beautifully designed breastplates graced their fronts. The rebbes stood around Reb Eliezer cradling the Torahs in their arms, as he began reciting the Kol Nidre. Three times the prayer would be said so that late-comers would hear it as well, softly the first time, louder the second, and still louder the third and final time.

Though we were permitted to sit for a good part of the service, many had chosen to stand. According to the Code of Jewish Law, one stood in order to resemble the angels. Everyone, however, rose for the Amidah, which on this night contained many extra prayers. I tried to absorb the meaning of every sentence, making certain I committed no errors in pronunciation, for this might, in some instances at least, alter the meaning of what I was saying. My heart was beating very quickly as I began reciting a long list of transgressions, hitting my breast with a clenched fist after each one:

. . . For the sin we committed against Thee by acting callously.

Oh, yes, I had done that, I thought, no need to dwell on it. Just don't do it again.

For the sin we committed in Thy sight unknowingly,
And for the sin we committed against Thee by idle talk.

How many times had I indulged myself in this manner? But would G-d believe that I was sincere in my entreaties to Him?

For the sin we committed in Thy sight by lustful behavior.

In the Yeshiva? Impossible. But wait. . . . What about the beautiful woman in the one movie I had seen? And then rushing on to the next one and the ones that followed it. Here was one I could admit to with ease:

And for the sin we committed against Thee intentionally and by mistake.

All I needed to do was be a man and own up to my imperfections. Our G-d was a merciful ruler. He would understand and forgive.

I had finished enumerating the first twenty sins. Then, summing up, I said:

And for all sins pardon us, G-d of forgiveness, and grant us atonement.

There were over forty types of sins to be confessed to, each one accompanied by a pounding of the breast. Every now and then I would feel as though I had said one without sufficient sincerity, and my guilt would compel me to repeat it with all the conviction I could muster.

Repentance was what G-d asked of us, but it was imperative that it be sincerely offered. G-d would know. Nothing could be hidden from him. We had learned that he who sinned thinking he would do penance on Yom Kippur would not gain forgiveness.

For two and a half hours we prayed like this, singing, chanting, whispering and thinking. No one said a word to his neighbor. Each must find his own path. Yet there was a most powerful, virtually unbreakable bond between us, for did we not worship the same Creator, follow the same laws, share a common dream, and strive for a common yet most uncommon understanding? Of course! And it was perhaps best exemplified by the song that we sang with joy several times:

> We are Thy people and Thou art our G-d,
> We are Thy children and Thou art our Father . . .
> We are Thy flock and Thou art our Shepherd. . . .

There was something warming about that last analogy, one that, in a funny way, made me sigh with relief. I could think of nothing more in need of protection than sheep. We were defenseless unless G-d was on our side. Moreover, by declaring ourselves to be in this state we were signifying not only awareness of our vulnerability but also our confidence in the Lord our shepherd.

After the service, I remained in the Beis haMedrash for a few hours, reading Psalms as was the custom on that night. There were some who stayed the whole night, alternating between reading and sleeping, but I did not consider myself to be on this level of sanctity and went to bed by 11 P.M.

The next day began early, just as it had on Rosh Ha-shonah, only this time we would not stop for lunch around 2 P.M. Rather, the entire day, from morning until evening, when three stars appeared in the sky, would be spent in the synagogue fasting and praying.

In all my life, I had never experienced such a day. At first, I simply devoted my energies to the prayers themselves. But as time passed, I began to feel a curious separation between myself and the words as they left my mouth. Perhaps it was the lack of food, perhaps it was the shimmering, swaying sea of white that surrounded me everywhere I turned, or perhaps it was the rising crescendo of voices led by Reb Eliezer. What I felt was that my words were traveling upward through the air, as if through constant repetition and sincerity of intention they could enter the Kingdom of G-d and reach the Holy Throne.

Reb Eliezer's words penetrated to the depths of my soul as he began chanting the story of the ten martyrs who had been tortured and put to death during the reign of Hadrian for having founded academies for the purpose of teaching Torah. As a child I had often wondered why, if G-d loved us so much, we were forced to suffer so, but now, after a year in the Yeshiva, I understood. That was the true test of our faith. G-d could not accept us until we had proven ourselves worthy of Him. Though I might spend hours questioning the interpretation of various passages in the Bible, I could never challenge the passages themselves. That was heresy. In fact, it was precisely because my mind functioned in a generally logical manner that my relationship to G-d was so special. It was the one area where I suspended all thought and judgement. That is not to say that I had no temptation to critically examine and evaluate my beliefs. I did, but I considered such an approach fundamentally wrong.

As morning turned into afternoon, there was no doubt in my mind that our prayers were being heard. The fervor that had taken hold of me had seized everyone else as well. As I paused in my prayers and looked around at the others, I felt embarrassed, for the intensity that was reflected in their movements and upon their faces seemed a most personal thing, something that ought to be witnessed only by the Lord Himself. I turned away quickly, hoping no one had noticed my worldly thoughts, but not before I had caught a glimpse of Rav Landau, tears streaming down his cheeks as he shook back and forth in rapid, staccato-like fashion. His expression, as he looked upward with outstretched arms, eyes shut tight, body clothed in garments of white, has remained vivid in my mind through the years. How I wished that I could have felt his passion, shared his devotion, seen his vision.

As the Holy Ark was opened for the Neilah (Concluding) Service, beads of sweat began to form on my brow. My hands felt clammy as I realized that after this final service, the last of five that were said on the Day of Atonement, my fate would be decided. As an indication of this we would now substitute the words "seal us" for "inscribe us" in the Book of Life whenever they appeared in the prayers. The Neilah Service lasted about an hour and fifteen minutes, with the Holy Ark remaining open and everyone standing. One would think that this might require great endurance coming at the end of a day of neither eating nor drinking, but in truth I hardly noticed. I had felt a little hungry the night before, but by now I could think only of what I was saying:

> Speedily open the Temple gates
> for those who value Thy Torah. . . .
>
> Speedily open heaven's gates
> for whose eyes are red from tears.

I found myself starting to weep, quietly at first, then uncontrollably as I allowed my pent-up emotions to come to the surface. My legs felt weak and I wanted to sit, but I could not while the Ark was open. I put one trembling hand on the chair in front of me. Gradually, I felt myself regaining control. The service was coming to an end, and as it did I slumped into my seat exhausted and emotionally drained. The long day was over.

Gradually I slipped back

into the everyday routine of Yeshiva life. I was in another class now. I had a new rebbe, Rav Speiser, and a new chavrusah, but my schedule was unchanged from the previous year. Every morning at 7 A.M. the cry "Shteht oif, shteht oif, l'avoidas haBoiray!" rang out through the morning stillness of the dormitory, and another day began. I prayed three times every day, studied for six or seven hours in the Beis haMedrash, and continued to celebrate the Sabbath and the holidays. Yet it was not the same.

At first I thought that my daily existence in the Yeshiva seemed unexciting only by comparison with the religious ecstasy of Rosh Hashonah and Yom Kippur, but as the weeks turned into months, I reconciled myself to the fact that this was, at best, a rationalization on my part.

In reality, a process of erosion was beginning. When I had met my old friends from elementary school, I had discovered that my own existence differed sharply from theirs, and that they did not hold my way of life in any great esteem. Then there was my contact with the boys at Camp Tikvath Shalom and the realization that they, too, were involved in other things. These were my friends, my peers, and I was not really different from them.

I found myself gazing with new-found interest at the news headlines as I waited in the local drugstore to pay for toothpaste, soap and other necessities. I began to linger there in order to catch a song or two on the radio. But this was minor, understandable as temptation. Of far greater significance was my reawakened interest in secular studies. As my geography teacher discussed life in faraway lands, such as India, China and Ethiopia, I was gripped by a desire to know more about them. Why did the people dress in a certain way? What were they like? What did they think of people like us?

I began to study history with greater interest, especially when my teacher talked about Germany's takeover of the Sudetenland. Yes, I thought, those were the same Germans who had caused so many in my family to perish. Here they were again, doing terrible things to Gentiles as well.

There was Mr. Patton, our English teacher, who labored to expose us to the writings of Shakespeare. The first year I had not been especially interested, but now I became perhaps his most receptive student. It was fascinating to read about Shylock, a member of my people, in *The Merchant of Venice,* and to be reminded by Shakespeare's portrait that throughout history our people had been regarded as outcasts by others. Mr. Patton towered over us, his long lanky frame resting against the blackboard as he called on us to read, correcting us whenever we failed to emphasize the proper words.

One day, as I sat in class, a vision flashed through my mind: Mrs. Harkness, my eighth-grade English teacher at Light of Abraham Yeshiva, a tiny woman with red-dyed hair made up in a bun, was standing in front of the room dressed in a gray skirt and frilly white blouse. She was praising me for a reading I had given from a portion of *Silas Marner.*

In that brief remembrance lay at least one clue to the change in attitude that was now emerging in me. My education before coming to Gates of Israel had been a liberal one. The value of secular knowledge had been impressed upon me in elementary school. Through the efforts of my teachers and from class trips to museums and plays I had learned to appreciate literature, art and science.

During my first year at Gates of Israel I had repressed such interests in favor of the Yeshiva's philosophy, but they had by no means been erased. They had merely lain dormant, and now that I was beginning to show greater interest in non-Talmudic matters, they returned stronger than ever, it seemed. I was not questioning the validity of the Talmud, for I had learned to love and respect it, not only at the Yeshiva but in my home as well. It was simply that I had become interested in other things, too.

At the same time, the fact that I had acquired additional interests affected the amount of time and energy I was able to give to the study of Torah. There were, after all, only so many hours to the day, and to spend more time on biology and geometry meant less time to devote to the Talmud. Of course, the rigid schedule required that I spend a certain amount of time reviewing the material covered in class by the rebbe, but whereas the previous year I had also devoted a good deal of my free time to studying Talmud, I now passed those hours absorbed in my new areas of interest.

Other matters began to influence me, too. There was a kosher grocery store near the Yeshiva, about two or three blocks away, where I sometimes went for a salami sandwich on a kaiser roll. The owners, a pleasant, modern-Orthodox, elderly couple, had a daughter about my age, who sometimes helped out behind the counter. I do not know how attractive she was to people outside the Yeshiva, but to me and a few friends in whom I dared confide, she was beautiful. Her name was Chana and she had long, deep-brown hair that hung loosely over a white apron. Her features were delicate: a thin small nose, long slender lips, high cheekbones, and luminous hazel-colored eyes, deep-set under a high forehead. Yet these observations were possible only when she was not looking directly at me, for when she did, I could feel myself redden and quickly turn away. I always tried to make certain that she, and not her parents, served me, thus giving me an opportunity to gaze longingly at her.

How I wished that I could think of something to say to her besides "Thank you" or "Please put some mustard on the roll." As a student at the Light of Abraham Yeshiva, I had talked to the girls in class without a trace of self-consciousness and had even gone out on a chaperoned date or two, but that was different. I recognized that the emotions and desires now churning inside me were those of an adult. Awareness of this both frightened and excited me. I found myself unable to speak to, yet unable to draw away from contact with, this girl who became the embodiment of my dreams and desires.

Fifteen-year-old boys are interested not only in girls. They like to play ball, go to movies and, in general, have fun. I found myself looking forward more than ever to those afternoons when I could be free to play ball and go swimming.

One Friday I took a long walk through a park located about two miles from the Yeshiva. Almost three months had elapsed since the High Holy Days. As I walked along the concrete paths flanked by sycamore, elm and maple trees, their fallen golden, yellow and red leaves forming a soft multicolored carpet, I felt a certain closeness to nature that had been absent in me for a long time. And what was wrong with that? I thought. Were these leaves and trees not G-d's creations? Was not the same true of the clear blue autumn sky and the pale white sun whose rays were casting deep shadows across my path?

My reverie was interrupted by shouting. As I rounded a curve in the path, I saw a group of boys in a field playing touch football. I stopped to watch them momentarily, but became absorbed in the game. Suddenly a tall, blond-haired boy with freckles across his nose yelled in my direction: "Hey you! Wanna play?" simultaneously throwing the football in my direction. It was a cold day and I was wearing a woolen knit cap over my head, instead of a skullcap, a coincidence which, I guess, made me look like any other teenager to them. I caught the ball, threw it back and before I knew it, I was in the game, running, throwing, tagging, shouting and laughing.

We must have played for over an hour before we all sank to the ground exhausted from our exertions. The last time I had enjoyed a game like that had been in the eighth grade on a class outing to Central Park. I lay spread-eagled on my back on the dry brown grass, looking up at the sky, taking in great gulps of cold, crisp air. To my left I could see the setting sun approaching the horizon.

The setting sun! How could I have forgotten? The Sabbath was coming and here I was lying on the ground in a park! I jumped up and, mumbling something about being expected home, began half-running, half-walking toward the Yeshiva. I could think of only one thing: "Don't be late." My weekly allowance of five dollars had come the day before and so I hailed a cab, using half of it to pay for the trip.

When I got to the Yeshiva, I was shaking. How could I have forgotten, even for a moment, what day it was?

Upsetting as this experience was, it did not really change anything. Though I still was fascinated by the Talmud, my attention wandered in class despite my best efforts to concentrate. The classroom was on the first floor, and its windows looked out over a quiet street whose peacefulness magnified every sound. An elderly lady walked by every day pushing a shopping cart whose creaking wheels were badly in need of oil. I grew to anticipate that sound, as well as that of the mailman emptying the large blue mailbox that stood at the corner, and that of the old man in the checked flannel shirt who watered his lawn every morning.

One day I became so absorbed looking at a sparrow chirping and preening itself on the branch of a nearby tree that I failed to hear Rav Speiser call on me to read. It was not until several moments had passed in complete silence that I noticed everyone staring at me. "Didn't you hear me call you, Naftoli?" demanded Rav Speiser. "Would it be too much trouble to ask you to read the Gemara?" "No," I murmured, embarrassed, and began explaining the progression of arguments raised by the various rabbis. Luckily for me, the boy on my left had a habit of always keeping his finger on the place or I would not have known where we were.

Afterward, as I was leaving for lunch, Rav Speiser stopped me. "Stay a moment, Naftoli, I want to talk with you," he said, motioning me to a chair. He was a thin, sallow-complexioned man in his mid-thirties with hollow cheeks, who was so tall that he was forced to bend his head slightly whenever he entered the classroom. Intense, humorless and extremely methodical in his teaching, he differed greatly from my first rebbe, Rav Landau. In his lectures, he took a step-by-step approach. Every question raised in class had to be within a given framework. His notes on the Talmud lay neatly in front of him, and those who sat near his desk could see on each page the precisely written numbers that identified the points he planned to make.

By contrast, Rav Landau had never used notes. He had

encouraged us to think creatively, to allow our minds to roam at will finding proofs in the Meforshim (Commentaries) and in other tractates of the Talmud. Rav Speiser assigned us specific Meforshim to read—a Rif, a Maharshah, the writings of Rabbi Akiba Aiger—but Rav Landau would simply say, "Look at the Meforshim, boys, and see what you can come up with." To Rav Landau it did not matter so much whether one's point was directly related to what we were learning. The question was: did it reflect imagination and depth? Rav Speiser was more concerned with accuracy and logical development and with making certain that we knew every single point backward and forward.

While I knew the importance of preciseness in understanding the Talmud, I found Rav Speiser's heavy emphasis on it uninspiring. If I could not relate to his derech (approach), how could I confide in him? And now we were alone in the room for the first time this year.

"Naftoli, what's bothering you? Why aren't you learning?" "I know the Gemara," I replied sullenly, picking at an imaginary thread near the side pocket of my black jacket. "That's not what I mean," said Rav Speiser. "I know you know the Gemara. That's not hard for someone with your capabilities. It's your lack of total involvement that concerns me. You're just going through the motions. Don't think you're fooling me," he added harshly.

How true that was. I had not been involved for months, and I knew it. In fact, I had been praying to G-d to help me rediscover the joy, the excitement, that had marked my endeavors when I first came to the Yeshiva. But those prayers had not been answered. I looked at Rav Speiser. I knew that he would not understand. He knew only one way—the one hundred percent way. Anything less was suspect.

"Look," he said, his voice suddenly taking on a cajoling

tone. "I want to help you, but I can't if you won't trust me. The yeitzer harah [evil spirit] affects everyone. You simply have to conquer it, and sometimes a person fails. Naftoli, I don't want you to fail. If you tell me what's disturbing you, maybe we can fight it together."

I began to feel uncomfortable. What he wanted me to do was bare my soul, to pour out my troubles to him. How could I? I knew he would not sympathize. Rav Landau would have been the right person, I felt, but he had left the Yeshiva and accepted a position at an institution in New York City.

"Let me try to do it myself, Rebbe," I finally said. "I need some more time to think. I want to work things out on my own." Rav Speiser looked at me rather coldly. I had rejected his offer and he sensed it. "Okay," he answered after a long silence. "If you change your mind, let me know." There were only fifteen minutes left for lunch. I rose and left the room.

Rav Speiser was not the only one who was aware of the changes I was undergoing. My classmates noticed it, too, and many of them stopped being friendly with me. They could not be friendly with someone who lacked their single-mindedness of purpose. Their rejection increased my sense of isolation.

The rebbe began calling on me to read only on rare occasions. I was no longer asked to lead the congregation in prayers and I was called up to the Torah less and less frequently.

There were others in the Yeshiva who had always been in the category into which I was now placed. They were hangers-on, whose stay in the Yeshiva was short-lived. But no one had expected much from them, and so the element of great disappointment was absent. In my case, however, it was more of a personal insult. I had the potential and I was not using it as they saw fit. In deciding to expend more energy on secular matters, I had challenged the Yeshiva's philosophy, for its approach stressed above all the need for total involvement that Rav Speiser had talked about—morning, noon and night, in both thought and action. Interest in secular matters could be justified by necessity, but not because it was valuable in and of itself. Not that the Yeshiva thought that science and mathematics, for example, were valueless; it was simply that they were not as valuable as Torah, and if one wanted to be a full-fledged member of the community, one could not spend much time on them.

This philosophy was most rigidly adhered to in the case of younger boys such as myself who, because of their age and lack of sophistication, were thought to be especially vulnerable to the temptations that surrounded us. The Yeshiva recognized that eventually the majority of its students would leave for the outside and so it wanted to make it possible for them to face that world from a position of strong conviction as upholders of the faith.

The torment I had experienced earlier in my efforts to know G-d was gone. I had come to accept the uncertainty that I believed was an integral part of faith. No, there was no clear break with the beautiful way of life that I had known since early childhood. There was simply a strong, overpowering desire to live in both worlds, a juggling act that those at the Gates of Israel Yeshiva would not accept as valid.

I attended quite a few movies that year—not so much because I enjoyed them, though I did, but more because I felt I had to prove something . . . that I could do things that were expressly prohibited by the Yeshiva and still lead a completely Orthodox way of life. I was indirectly challenging their notion of the need for complete immersion in the spiritual world. The problem was that I was still very much a part of that world. I could not forget my first year and the fact that I had never known such joy and ecstasy as when I had been studying the Talmud with "all my heart and soul." Yet, although I wanted to recapture that feeling, I could not bring myself to give up my attachment to science, math and English. Nor could I put other nonacademic yearnings out of my mind.

Such a situation could not continue indefinitely. I made an appointment to see Reb Eliezer. In reality, I no longer had much hope of resolving what I had come to believe was an impossible situation, but I felt an obligation to try. My meeting with him was scheduled, ironically enough, for 2:30 P.M., which was the beginning of a short break we had between our Talmud and secular studies classes.

As I knocked on the door to his office, I was seized by a desire to run away, but it was too late. He had already opened the door. I walked in and waited until he returned to his seat behind the scarred and chipped oak desk. It was a small room with a musty odor, crowded with bookcases on whose shelves stood hundreds of holy books, their worn and cracked bindings concealing pages yellowed with age.

"Why did you want to see me?" asked Reb Eliezer in Yiddish. I cleared my now dry throat awkwardly several times before speaking.

"It's about my learning," I began in a faltering tone. "Reb Eliezer, is it wrong to be interested in secular studies if you can keep up with the Gemara?"

"That's a relative statement, Naftoli," he answered. "Assuming you are keeping up with the Gemara, that only proves that without the distraction of such studies you would do much better, *as you did your first year here, Naftoli.*"

His answer was like a stab at my heart. I knew that he was aware of what was happening to me, but he spoke in such a condescending tone. I rushed on. "But many Orthodox Jews study both. I can't help it. I want to learn more about the rest of the world, too. Why is that not possible?"

Reb Eliezer paused before answering. "Possible?" he said, mimicking me. "Of course it's possible. But not here at the Gates of Israel Yeshiva!" Then his voice suddenly turned soft. "You know where it's possible? In New York. There are plenty of yeshivas where you can study both to your heart's content, if that's what you want. There is even a place where you can go to college and learn Gemara under the same roof. They call it synthesis, I think. I call it something else, but what difference does it make what I call it? If you want to go there, I can't stop you."

I was frightened half out of my wits. I had never seen him so upset. Protesting, I said that the rebbe had misunderstood me. But it was to no avail. He looked at me with a sad expression, his unfocused eyes underscoring the distance that now separated us. "Naftoli, I wish you the best of luck whatever you decide." And then, with a wave of his hand, he dismissed me.

For the next few days, I walked around dazed. My humiliation was compounded by the suspicion that others knew what had happened, for a few boys had been standing in the hallway near the door as I left and it would have been difficult for them not to have overheard our voices. I knew I could no longer stay.

I wrote to my father. How could I explain to him why the infectious enthusiasm with which I had studied the Talmud in my first year at the Yeshiva seemed to have dissipated?

I could not even explain it clearly to myself. All I knew was that I had to leave. I tried to include all the factors I believed had played a role—the interest I had developed in other things, especially secular subjects, my liberal Orthodox upbringing, the departure of Rav Landau whom I had revered, the influence of my friends during the summer. True, I wrote my father, many boys did not leave the Yeshiva and a few even spent their entire lives there, but I could speak only for myself. I hoped he would understand and not be too disappointed.

The answer came a few days later, full of compassion and wisdom. My father wanted me to know that, above all, he loved me, and that if I was unhappy, he was unhappy. He had seen the change that came over me during the summer but assumed that everything would straighten out when I returned to the Yeshiva. As to my interest in secular studies —well, he wanted to tell me a story:

When I first came to this country in 1946 after the war, I met a man whom I had known in Lancut, Poland, where I grew up. "Let's have lunch together," he said, "and talk about old times." I agreed and we went to a nearby dairy restaurant. Upon seeing that I went to the back of the restaurant to wash for bread, he exclaimed "Helmreich, you're still religious? Don't be silly! This is America and the world is going forward. You'll see—in five years men will be on the moon and no one will believe in G-d anymore!"

And now, Willy, fifteen years have passed since that day. We have not reached the moon, but we have gone into outer space and man still believes in G-d—for every discovery shows man how much he does not know and how full of mystery the universe is. If you want to study science and other subjects, I'm not afraid for you because in the end everything comes back to the Creator of the world anyway, the one who makes all knowledge, secular and religious, possible.

The person in the world who meant the most to me still believed in me. I went to Rav Eisen, the head administrator of the high school division and formally notified him of my decision. "I know," he said. "Your father called me last night and told me you are leaving. He also asked me to tell you that he has enrolled you in a yeshiva in Brooklyn. They do not stress the study of the Talmud as much as we do, but I think it is a fine school, and maybe it's all for the best. Good luck to you." He had been kind to me. We did not know each other well and perhaps this made it easier for him. I thanked him and went upstairs to pack my bags. I would leave the following day.

The next morning after breakfast I said goodbye to my friends—Zevulun, Yehuda, Yitzchak and a few others. Our feelings of discomfort were mutual. I had known great happiness here, but no longer would I be a part of their world. The road I was taking was, in their eyes, fraught with peril, and once I had chosen it, no one could tell where it might end. It was one thing to disagree with their way of life as an outsider, but to have been a part of that community and to leave was a different matter entirely. None of this was said aloud. It did not have to be. I knew what they were thinking.

I called a cab and went downstairs to wait in front of the building. As I headed out the door, I could hear the sounds of learning coming from the Beis haMedrash. Suddenly there was a lump in my throat as I stood alone in the vestibule by the door, unable to move, mesmerized by the familiar singsong tone.

"Did you call for a cab?" said a voice somewhere behind me. "Oh, yes," I said, "I'm coming. Can you give me a hand with these bags, please?" I stepped outside and went slowly down the long walk to the car.

In twenty minutes we were at the station. The bus was

already waiting. I boarded quickly, and as we pulled out of the departure area, my lips began to move:

May it be Thy will, Lord our G-d and G-d of our fathers, to lead us in safety and to direct our every step in safety.

May Thou bring us to our destination in life, happiness and peace.

Save us from every enemy and ambush and from all the thieves and wild animals that lurk on the road and from all afflictions that visit and trouble the world.

Send a blessing upon the work of Thy hands.

Let me acquire grace, loving-kindness and mercy in Thine eyes and in the eyes of all who see us.

Hear our pleas, for Thou art the Lord, who listens to our prayers and to our pleas.

Blessed art Thou, O Lord, who hears our prayers.